*A Lady's Experiences
in the Wild West in 1883*

A
Lady's
Experiences
IN THE
Wild West
IN *1883*

by
Rose Pender

Foreword by
A. B. Guthrie, Jr.

University of Nebraska Press
Lincoln/London

First Bison Book printing: 1985
Most recent printing shown by first digit below:
1   2   3   4   5   6   7   8   9   10

Library of Congress Cataloging in Publication Data
Pender, Rose, Lady.
  A lady's experiences in the Wild West in 1883.

  Reprint of the 1888 ed. published by G. Tucker, London.
  1. The West—Description and travel—1880–1950.
2. United States—Description and travel—1865–1900.
3. Pender, Rose, Lady. I. Title.
F595.P38 1978   978'.02   78–17690
ISBN 0-8032-8711-9

Contents

Foreword

Even students of the West are unlikely to recognize the name Rose Pender, and less likely to know her book, *A Lady's Experiences in the Wild West*, published five years after her adventures in 1883. I seem to recall from my reading a vague reference or two to the book and the authoress (her word), but nothing definite lies in my memory. The volume itself is so rare as to be almost inexistent.

But now comes the University of Nebraska Press with a reprint that all students and collectors will want. It deals with a West in transition from frontier to the glimmer of modern times, from open range to fenced pastures, from trails to trains, from makeshift and make-do to more convenient and easier ways. We see it through the eyes and from the sensibilities of a gentlewoman and a Britisher to boot.

The woman was indeed a Lady. She brought to America her highborn prejudices and standards—a dislike of the Irish, a distaste for blacks, and a revulsion to dirt—and with them a sharp eye, a chatty pen, and a game spirit.

An untrustworthy reporter, one might presume, a person class-bound and blind to initiative, necessarily rude and unlikely ever to accommodate herself to the ways of a developing America.

On most counts the presumption would be wrong.

In company with two men and sometimes more— one her husband, and the other, we must conclude, his business associate—she traveled from New York to Washington, to St. Louis, San Antonio, Los Angeles, San Francisco, Lake Tahoe, Carson City, Reno, Salt Lake City, Cheyenne, Denver, Fort Laramie, Rapid City, Spearfish, Miles City, and then back to the East Coast. En route they made numerous side trips, one to Pike's Peak, reached by foot through deep snow. For transport they used trains, horse-drawn vehicles and, more than once, their own feet.

At Cheyenne she assumed she had ended her trip through the "civilized" portion of the United States. She enjoyed Cheyenne, and no wonder. In the town and at the Cheyenne Club she must have met people of her own station. The settlement was central to the operations of the huge range-cattle ranches of upper-class Britons and Scotsmen, and the Cheyenne Club was metropolitan enough for high-title tastes. Her husband had some interests in ranching, too, before the lethal winter of 1886–87 put an end to foreign hopes of profit.

From Cheyenne she attended a roundup on the "Platt" River. She and her companions forded rivers in flood, got stuck in mud holes, went without food and sometimes without water, crossed risky passages, lost their way in the dark, endured blazing sun and night storm. If she was dismayed, she was never defeated.

The Lady complained, without ever whining, about dirt, dirty hotel rooms, dirty trains, dirty houses and cabins, dirty people, and dirty meals. She was revolted by bugs in her bed. She was right, of course. The frontier hadn't time, even given the wish, for cleanliness and disinfectants, and fastidiousness wasn't according to custom.

Yet she was alive to the beauties of the country, to spring flowers and sunsets and morning dew. When she met people she liked, highborn or not, or ate food that pleased her, she was quick to say so. American bread was always uncommonly excellent.

It is in her sharp observations that the book has its interest and values. The ways of daily life in city and country caught her eye, and here are reported. Her criticisms have point beyond any prejudices. She adds to our knowledge of a time no one is old enough to remember.

What finally were her feelings? In summing up she was able to state, as against any complaints: "And so ends the record of our most enjoyable fourth months' travels through the United States. We had seen, 'done,' and gone through as varied an experience as was possible in the time—an experience that I shall always look back upon as one of the most enjoyable of my life."

A. B. GUTHRIE, JR.

Publisher's Preface

Except for the occasional breaking up of long paragraphs and the addition of chapter titles and a couple of explanatory footnotes (in brackets), Rose Pender's narrative of her experiences in the Wild West in 1883 is presented here as nearly as possible in its pristine form. Misspellings such as "Waho" for "Waco," "River Beagas" for "Brazos," "Oatlands" for "Oakland," and "Truchi" for "Truckee" (to list only a few) have not been corrected, for her eccentric rendering of names is as much a part of her character—and the fun of the book—as her tart comments on western life or her account of marching intrepidly up Pikes Peak, trusty umbrella in hand.

Rose Pender and her husband, James (she became Lady in 1897, when he was created a baronet) were part of a horde of Britishers who flocked to the Great American West in the latter half of the nineteenth century as hunters, journalists, investors, or simply curiosity seekers. The Penders were already seasoned travelers in the best Victorian tradition, having toured African ports five years earlier. The title of Rose's book about that trip—*No Telegraph; or, A Trip to Our Unconnected Colonies in 1878*—reflects family business interests: her father-in-law, John Pender, was largely responsible for the laying of the trans-Atlantic cable and, later, the construction of the telegraph system that linked England with her Eastern empire. Rose frequently alludes to countrymen who were also touring the West or had recently done so. She was obviously familiar with Isabella Bird's story of her 1873 visit, *A Lady's Life in the Rocky Mountains*, and, in the middle of the Wyoming prairie, she encountered Moreton Frewen, an uncle of Winston Churchill who managed a cattle ranch from headquarters on the Powder River.

The chance meeting with Frewen is really not surprising. Large numbers of foreigners—especially Englishmen and Scotsmen—invested in the range cattle industry until the grazing of cattle on Indian lands in present-day Oklahoma was restricted by the government and the severe winter of 1886–87 caused heavy losses. At the very time that Rose and James Pender were inspecting the cattle enterprise they had invested in, a representative of John Pender, Gregor Lang, was establishing a cattle ranch on the Little Missouri in present North Dakota. (Two years later James Pender would join the Little Missouri roundup crew, which included a neighboring rancher, a young New Yorker by the name of Theodore Roosevelt. On this occasion James was reportedly offended by the cowboys' refusal to address him as "Mister" and annoyed the cook by taking along his own alcohol stove and supply of concentrated soup.)

As for the Penders' careers after the loss of their ranching investments, John of cable company fame was knighted in 1888 and received many other honors, including the designation of the county seat of Thurston County, Nebraska, as Pender because of his position as a director of the railroad that served the town. James continued his father's business interests, served as a Conservative M.P., indulged his hobbies of hunting and yachting, and died in 1921 in his eightieth year. Rose—a doughty old lady, one can imagine—survived her husband by eleven years.

A Lady's Experiences
in the Wild West in 1883

Preface

As so many years have elapsed since I wrote the little history of our trip through the Wild West, I feel I must now write a short preface to explain what might otherwise appear a series of mis-statements. The changes that have taken place between 1883 and 1888 would appear little short of marvellous did we not know how rapidly things alter, disappear and improve in America.

For instance, where only a few years ago such a visitation was deemed improbable, if not utterly impossible, a railroad has now been made right through the best of the cattle-raising country, bringing with it gangs of grangers (or farmers) and emigrants. Tracts of land have been taken up, fences run for miles, water rights disputed, and the unhappy cattle rancheman has been slowly, but surely, driven off.

Then the collapse of the gigantic Indian Territory cattle scheme—through reasons which I cannot give here, as it would be opening too wide a question for me to venture an opinion upon—flooded the ranges with vast herds of cattle. Where, during our tour, we complained of the long sweeps of rich pasture with hardly a head of cattle to be seen, now the grass is literally eaten down to the root. A succession of such severe winters as were not even taken into consideration have decimated the herds. Scarcity of food has done the rest; and happy, indeed, is the owner of cattle who can safely count on only 50 or 60 per cent. of loss. The cattleman is looking sadly forlorn, and asks himself why such persistent ill-luck has pursued him.

The price of beef has been systematically kept down, so that profit by this means is stopped. The loss of calves by the late cold springs has been terrible, and I believe we may safely consider that the number of cattle in the West is reduced by some 50 per cent. all through. This is very depressing, no doubt; still there is always some silver lining, however black the cloud. The price of beef and also of cattle must rise, and those ranchemen who have saved a portion of their stock may hope to realise almost as good a profit from their remaining herds as they would have done with twice the number a year ago. There is still a future for cattle owners—a future, be it remarked, I do not say a fortune.

Like most industries now-a-days, especially agricultural ones, by good management and hard work a living is to be made by them, but the good old time of fortune-making has gone by. There is too much competition over everything, and it becomes a difficulty to live.

As I have often been asked, What is a Round-up? I will, in a few words, explain it. In plain English,

a Round-up is a search or hunt in the spring for all
the cattle in the locality. Several owners join
together. An outfit, which consists of waggons drawn
by mules, a large herd of horses, and as many men
from each owner as is necessary, is assembled, under
the command of a headman or foreman. The country
is systematically scoured for miles, sometimes for
hundreds of miles. All the cattle collected are driven
to some settled locality, when the calves are branded,
and the beeves destined for market are driven off, a
rough estimate of profit or loss is made out, and when
this part of the business is finished the Round-up
terminates, and the men depart to their ranches.
There is usually an autumn Round-up for the fat
oxen and the late calves, but this is not so important
as the calf Round-up in the spring.

Having offered this short apology for the many
discrepancies that will, no doubt, be discovered
between my assertions of "then" and the facts of
"now," I throw myself on the kindness and for-
bearance of my readers, and subscribe myself their
very humble Servant,

THE AUTHORESS.

March, 1888.

CHAPTER I

From New York to Cheyenne

It was a cold, dull morning when the "Servia" came into her berth in the North River and we touched American ground for the first time. We had had a remarkably fine passage for the time of year, and made the voyage in seven and a half days from Queenstown. It had been rough at times and very cold, especially off Newfoundland, where we sighted several icebergs. I think we were all very glad to be on shore, for a voyage across the Atlantic in the month of March is not a pleasure trip. My first impression of New York was certainly not a favourable one, and the frightful confusion and scrambling for luggage in the huge shed-like edifice where all the contents of the "Servia" were thrown down pell-mell, without the least regard to letters or numbers, did not lessen it, anything worse managed being impossible to conceive. It was a hunt amongst hundreds of boxes and cases for one's own especial property, and when this was found the weary passenger had to drag his or her box or portmanteau to where he or she proposed to form their pile, and then continue the search till by degrees all the belongings are secured. Then another hunt for an officer to examine the luggage; and, for a free country, this search is anything but a form. Woe betide you if you have a suspiciously new-looking dress or jacket at the top of your box. You will then have all your goods turned topsy turvy, in spite of all protestations. I was told that a gold piece or two might help to lessen the zeal of the Custom House servants, but that it was a dangerous thing to attempt, as there were spies constantly on the look out for officers accepting bribes; so we allowed events to take their course.

Thanks principally to our friend Mr. W——d, of the Direct United States Cable Company, we escaped very easily, and about two hours after leaving the ship we found ourselves bumping over the New York pavement *en route* to the Brevoort House. The distance could not have been much over two miles, but the modest charge made by our hack driver was five dollars. Cab hire is very extravagant in New York, and either on this account, or perhaps owing to the terrible state of the pavements, which really makes driving a painful experience, very few people employ the cabs; tram-cars, the elevated railroad, or even an omnibus is preferred.

Of course, my husband was interviewed even before he left the ship, and though he really barely answered his interrogator beyond what civility demanded, next morning a column and a half was taken up in the *Morning Journal* detailing the remarks and opinions that had "not" been elicited from him.

We had very comfortable rooms at the Brevoort, which is a first-class hotel, and certainly as good a restaurant as could be found anywhere. That the charges are excessive is only a natural sequence, but that the whole place should be kept so unbearably heated by hot air was, to me, a far more serious grievance. It was really cruel. One could hardly breathe anywhere inside, and my only alternative to being roasted was to turn off the hot air and sit in my bedroom and shiver, as it was bitterly cold outside and the snow was falling fast.

New York society was in a state of pleasurable excitement when we arrived anent a huge fancy ball to be given by the Vanderbilts, which was to come off that night, and which turned out a most successful affair. The dresses were superb. I saw one or two that were really most beautiful, and were made in New York; but, of course, most of the costumes came from Paris.

I will not describe our stay in this gay city, but I must gratefully acknowledge the kindness and hospitality that was shown us by everyone. We only remained in New York a few days, but quite long enough to feel "at home" with several charming families. I was taken to most of the places of special interest, and generally made "free of the City" in the pleasantest manner possible, and in the kindest company. We felt really sorry to move on, but our time was limited, and we had rather to "rush it."

We left for Washington on the 3rd of April, and this was my first acquaintance with the mode of American railway travelling. I am forced to own I disliked it. The absence of porters to carry one's bags, &c., the hurry, and, oh! the fearful heat of the carriages into which one is thrust, amongst a crowd of fellow sufferers, is horrid. There is no privacy, or comfort, or quiet; the conductors keep marching through demanding to look at the tickets every half-hour or so, and their habit of banging the doors at each end becomes maddening; then come fruit, candy, and book sellers, apparently at their own sweet wills, pestering one to buy, sometimes laying a book or sample of their goods on your lap, by way, I suppose, of inducing the unwary to commit themselves. Every window is fast shut, and if we ventured to open one near us savage looks and stern requests from the conductor to close it, on account of some lady or child being "sick," greeted us at once, and if we insisted on keeping a portion of it open a general stampede took place to seats at a distance from the partly opened window. I think Americans as a rule have as great a dread of fresh air as the Germans, and the general "stuffiness" that pervaded all their arrangements was very trying to me all through our wanderings.

Washington is about seven hours by rail from New York, and we left the latter place at three in the afternoon. It was too dark to see anything as we drove to Wormsley's Hotel. Mr. and Mrs. Hubbard, who are old friends and met us at the station, kindly took me in their own carriage, and Jamie, Bob, and Mr. E. Beaumont all followed in the omnibus. Our luggage arrived shortly afterwards, having been "expressed" to the hotel. This system of delivery of luggage is excellent in theory, but in practice it requires better management. Such a system would not work where the passenger traffic was very heavy. You "express" your luggage to the hotel at which you have decided to stay; the expressman and his vehicle come for the goods, and gives you a large medal with a number attached for each package. If you have many packages your pocket becomes very heavy with the medals. Before reaching your journey's end another expressman comes "on board," takes your checks away and gives you others, which you retain till your luggage is delivered. If you lose a check you are in danger of losing the package, or it sometimes happens that you get a wrong medal, and then you find you have some one else's bag or bundle instead of your own, which is trundling away towards San Francisco—or somewhere. Another drawback is the delay in delivery. Hours sometimes elapse before the luggage arrives, and after a long dreary journey, when one is anxious to get to bed or obtain a change of raiment, it is most annoying, to say nothing of one's natural anxiety for the safety of the luggage. On the whole, I much prefer the English method, and taking my boxes, &c., away on my own cab.

Wormsley's Hotel is kept by a coloured man, and all the waiters, serving-maids, &c., are coloured. It is a very comfortable hotel, though plain and homely in its arrangements; the black waiters are very civil and obliging, but terribly slow. The black man's intellect is far slower than his white brother's, and it takes considerable patience to get him to understand what you mean; but he is good-tempered and jolly, and I like him far better than the pretentious half-breed, who is, as a rule, sulky and disagreeable.

Washington is a charming city; so well planned and laid out, and so beautifully clean. The streets are chiefly paved with asphalte, and are kept in good order. I mention this particularly, as the want of well-paved streets is a striking feature in most large American towns. The Capitol, which answers to our

Houses of Parliament, stands on a hill. It is prettily constructed of white marble, and is an imposing structure. The inside strikes one as poor and tawdry. I had my attention particularly drawn to some huge paintings representing the defeat of the English troops, and pourtraying various British disasters of the year of Independence. I did not feel at all hurt. As our national victories are so numerous, the record of a defeat is almost a relief.

I think the American soldiers are better taken care of when past work than our own warriors. We drove through "The Rest," as the soldiers' home is called. Such a pretty park, and so well kept. I saw a number of superannuated warriors sitting about in the woods or basking in the sun, in little groups, smoking and talking; and very happy they all seemed. We also visited the soldiers' graveyard, where many thousands lie buried. Each grave is marked by a headstone with the name and age, or a simple number in cases where the body had not been recognized before interment. Northern and Southern are, I believe, buried together, and every year there is a commemoration day, when these graves are visited by thousands of persons, who bring flowers to lay on the tombs. It is a pretty idea, is it not? and worthy of extended imitation amongst ourselves.

The weather was delightfully warm and quite different to that of New York, which city we left in a snowstorm; but I noticed that vegetation was not as forward as it was in England when we left. A month, however, makes a great change in America, and everything bursts into flower and leaf as if by magic. We spent two very pleasant evenings at a friend's house, and made the acquaintance of some notable and agreeable people. We also spent a day at

Baltimore, but were disappointed in the appearance of the city.

Our next move was to St. Louis. We had the usual struggle and bother about our luggage at the station, but fortunately our party was both strong and energetic, and after a hard but successful fight to get to our car, we finally settled ourselves and our belongings and started on our picturesque journey. It was extremely lovely when we began to climb up the 1,900 feet to the top of the Alleghanies—all rock, forest, and river. We sometimes seemed to hang over the precipice, like flies on a wall, and could see the muddy torrent below us careering among huge timber trees, for we were now in the land of the lumberer. Not a vestige of animal life to be seen anywhere, for the winters are too long and too severe for even the hardier animals to exist. Once in a way we passed a small station house, and the four or five inhabitants all assembled to see us go by, evidently the one event of the day. A mail bag was thrown out but no stoppage took place. Our two engines climbed steadily and slowly up, puffing hard, as if they found it all they could do to drag us. Great clumps of rhododendrons clothed the steep sides of the hills. In the spring these beautiful plants must present a very gay appearance amongst the dark pines.

Here I must enter another protest against the American's apparent dislike of light and comfort. The windows of our drawing room car were so small and low that we lost a great part of the beauty of the scenery. However, in defiance of the rules, some of us stood outside on the little platform, where we could see very well, as ours was the rear car.

It got dark shortly after six, and after making some tea by means of a spirit lamp we settled down to one

11

quiet rubber, which proceeded as well as the jolting of the car would permit. Shortly after, seeing that all the beds in the Pullman had been made up, and that our porter was looking very wistfully at us, we allowed him to settle ours, and we all crept in to our coffin-like berths, dressed as we were, and endeavoured to sleep. It was a long night, and I never closed my eyes; the fearful closeness and discomfort of being boxed up with three other persons in so confined a space rendered sleep impossible. I think we were all very thankful when daylight came and we were able to get up.

We reached Cincinnati about six o'clock, and were all bustled out on to a long and very dirty platform. Of course, we had to carry our own goods and chattels, as in these regions a porter is an unknown luxury. As we are accustomed when at home to have things fairly comfortable, we found it really no joke to carry dressing bags, bundles of rugs and carpet bags for a long distance in the midst of a jostling crowd of very rough people. A huge four-horse omnibus was waiting to take us to the other station. Here we had to wait an hour in the bitter cold. We obtained some coffee and a roll for breakfast at a very dirty restaurant, and were told by the proprietors of this wretched place that we should not stop anywhere for refreshment before one o'clock, and neither did we; but there was a dining-car attached to our train when it came up and a luxurious breakfast was spread, which was rather aggravating to our feelings, seeing that we had already breakfasted, albeit badly.

Cincinnati was completely flooded the February before our arrival, and the conductor showed us the water mark, some ten feet high. The country round was still swamped, and much of it was under water. We travelled in a "day" Pullman, which is a much pleasanter car than those used for night service, as it is possible to look out of the windows. The arm-chairs in the day cars are easier than the back-breaking arrangement which in the night car is converted into a bed. The objection, however, previously urged, of the porter or conductor constantly walking past, and the banging of doors every few minutes, is very annoying, and no rest or peace is obtainable.

We reached St. Louis at half-past six o'clock the following day, and thinking we had actually arrived at our destination, and as everyone seemed to be getting out, Mr. B—— and J—— jumped out and began to hand down the luggage, when, without the least notice, on went the train, leaving us looking extremely silly. We were complacently informed that we were more than a mile from the railway depôt, and had to scramble through the very muddiest streets I ever saw before we reached the depôt. The only trap we could get was a thing resembling a pig cart, with a bench behind the driver's seat and straw scattered at the bottom. It was not quite a mile to the hotel, but the driver charged us a dollar and a-half. We were so anxious to get to comfortable quarters after our thirty hours' journey in the cars that we paid without dispute, which, indeed, is quite useless, as the Jehu adheres to his tariff, however exorbitant.

We put up at the Southern Hotel, which is always spoken of by Americans as being as near perfection as possible. It is very cleverly planned, and well built as far as the public rooms go, but the bed rooms are not good, being either very stuffy or too large, and we found the attendance was very bad. The dining rooms hold some hundred people, and it is impossible to get attended to. Soup is first placed on the table, and then an interval takes place of twenty minutes at least before the fish appears—and so on. Let me offer a word of advice to those who purpose staying at an American hotel. It is worse than useless to appear annoyed, as this only delights the dusky waiter, and he will be even slower than is his wont. If he sees you bear the annoying delay good temperedly, or as if you did not notice it, he will hurry up to get through with the service, but the unfortunate who begins to fret and fume had better make up his mind at once to quit, and forfeit the meal. America is such a free country for those who undertake contracts and do not feel inclined to properly fulfil them.

After dinner, during which two of our party quite lost all patience, we went to the theatre to see "Taken from Life." It was a funny sight, as the men spectators sat in their shirt sleeves, and there were hardly any women in the place. It was the work-man's night *par excellence*, and I felt a little *de trop*. The audience was wonderfully quiet and orderly, except when the villain of the piece came on before the curtain after the second act. The way he was hooted and yelled at was almost alarming, and I felt sorry for him.

Dr. Carson, who had heard from his father that we were coming to St. Louis, came at once to call on us. The next day being Sunday we felt somewhat surprised to see a number of shops open and the traffic going on much as on week days. We drove all about the city under Dr. Carson's guidance, and saw a capital match of base ball going on between two clubs. It is a pretty game, and I wonder it is not more in vogue in England. We then drove to see the wonderful bridge over the Mississippi. It is a marvel of engineering skill and energy, though, of course, the Brooklyn bridge has since put it in the shade. We also went on board one of those floating palaces, a Mississippi river steamer. It was starting on its first voyage, and everything was deliciously clean and pretty. Such dear little state rooms, nicely fitted up, and a beautiful saloon. There were three decks to the vessel, and the decorations were snow white, picked out with gold. She was to start the next day for New Orleans, with a full complement of passengers.

By far the most interesting sight we saw in St. Louis was the fire brigade at exercise. Dr. Carson had arranged with the head of the department for a private show for our entire benefit. The fire office is a good sized building. The engines are placed in rows on each side of the shed, with the stables at the back. We first saw the men go through their exercise. By means of hooks, five or six men in a wonderfully short time climb from the outside to the top of an eight-storey house. It is very simply contrived, but most effective, and the men are certainly smart. The horses, however, distance them in quickness and intelligence. They stand in loose boxes with their heads to the entrance—of course, ready harnessed; a chain passes in front of the row of boxes, and when the alarm bell rings by means of some electric contrivance this chain drops down. At once the horses, who perhaps are slumbering peacefully, dash out in their order, and, with shrieks of delight, come tearing down the narrow way between the fire engines, each horse placing himself ready to be "hitched up" to his own engine. I am not quite sure, but I think *fifteen seconds* is the time allowed for the men to rise and be ready with their engines. They

15

sleep above the fire engine shed, but instead of a staircase there is a smooth wooden pillar down which they slide. The number of fires is very great in St. Louis, as so many houses are built of wood, and since Chicago was burnt down special attention is paid all over the United States to the fire brigades. They certainly are wonderfully well drilled, and all the arrangements are as nearly perfection as is possible. It was only natural, under the circumstances, that my thoughts should turn homeward. I wonder if it will be necessary for us to receive a similar lesson to that of Chicago before we put "our house in order" in the matter of the fire brigade service.

I was taken all over the St. Louis Hospital by our kind friend, and was much pleased with the building—the wards are so large, cool, and clean. The nurses, in their high white caps and spotless aprons, were moving about noiselessly, and the poor patients seemed as well cared for as they could be. It is not a large place but well situated.

The drives through the park and public gardens of St. Louis are very pretty, and there is excellent snipe shooting to be had outside the town. There is also a pack of foxhounds, and had we stayed a day or two longer we should have had an opportunity of comparing American fox-hunting with our own. We were, however, anxious to proceed on our journey, so, after attempting to get some dinner at our hotel—an effort that the coloured waiters entirely frustrated by keeping us waiting even longer than usual—we drove to the station, and got our goods checked through to San Antonio. Although we had allowed half-an-hour extra to get this done, we nearly lost our train after all, as we had to get our luggage to the car as best we could, and it was by no means an edifying

16

spectacle to see me mounting guard over our possessions while the men folk went backwards and forwards. The train was actually on the move before we obtained our tickets. Certainly there is a great deal yet for the Americans to learn in the way of railway travelling and accommodation, and I would seriously urge upon their railway magnates the advisability of sending a few picked officials to England to study the English railway and luggage arrangements. The experience gained would, I am sure, greatly add to the comfort of their customers.

It was late enough when we got "on board" to order our beds to be made up, and as this was a two nights' journey I persuaded myself to undress, which I found makes the journey much less fatiguing. We awoke in the Indian territory, and I had been led to expect we should find this part of the country very lovely. Unfortunately we were too early for the flowers, and the trees were only beginning to bud. It struck me as being a flat and uninteresting country, covered with scrubby trees, and studded with wide, shallow brooks. Plenty of rolling prairie covered with rich grass, but the land little under cultivation. We passed through many Indian villages, composed of some dozen or even fewer wooden shanties. The squaws, with their papooses, stared stolidly at us. Here and there we met a (no doubt) great chief, riding, bare-backed, a very little mustang. At one small station we actually saw four "braves" engaged in the exhilarating game of croquet. Shade of Uncas, what would you think of this!

I was greatly disappointed in the red men; they are an insignificant and ugly race. A great many had the lowest Irish type of features, and were vastly inferior in strength to the Zulu and in grace to the coolie or

17

Tamil. They appear a squalid, cruel and degraded people.

We left St. Louis on the 10th of April, and before we reached our destination the climate had changed considerably. It was very, very hot, and so dusty that everything one touched or tasted was gritty. The jolting of the train, which travelled very slowly, prevented one being able to write at all, or read without effort. So the day dragged on wearily.

On the morning of the 11th of April we entered the State of Texas—a fine rolling grass country, well watered. We saw thousands of sheep grazing on the hilly slopes. Texas offers great advantages for cattle raising, as the winters are not so severe here as they are further north, and therefore the percentage of loss at calving time is not so great. The cattle are, however, liable to what is called Texan fever, and sometimes from this cause the mortality is very great. Texan cattle driven up to Wyoming or Nebraska do not at present seem to carry this disease with them, and the breed shows a great improvement after a year or so of the keener air. The Texan cattle are a poor, straggling-looking lot with very wide horns, and this is against them greatly, as they are so apt to injure each other on their way by rail to the northern markets. The Texan summers are very hot, and sometimes a scarcity of water will destroy a good range. On the whole, notwithstanding bad winters and calving losses, I should much prefer to herd cattle in the more northern districts. The latter loss will, I believe, be remedied to a great extent in the future by enclosing the ranges. In the northern districts, too, the climate is much healthier, and time can be passed much more pleasantly, as there is a fair amount of sport with deer and antelope.

We stopped at Waho, a neat little town of some 5,000 inhabitants. Four years ago it consisted of a dozen persons. The best building here is the Court House, and there is an exceedingly pretty suspension bridge over the River Beagas. I noticed a deal of land under cultivation, and the cotton, Indian corn, and other crops looked very well. I saw the snake fence here for the first time; it is very ingenious, and would prove a nasty obstacle in the hunting-field.

We reached San Antonio at half-past eight on the 12th, very wearied of our forty-eight hours' confinement in the cars. A lumbering four-horse, covered brake was waiting at the station, into which every one was hustled. When quite full we started and made the tour of the town, stopping at the different hotels to put down passengers. Our hotel, Manenk's, was the last on the list—a small dirty place, with the inevitable bar below. We asked a woman who was standing at the door of the parlour if the telegram sent on by us to Mrs. Manenk had arrived, and if our rooms were ready. "I am Mrs. Manenk, but I don't know anything of your telegram," was the ungracious reply, and she walked off in a huff. After some trouble, a waiter was discovered, who told us our wire had arrived, and we were shown into a bed room on the sunny side of the house, which was close and stuffy in consequence. It was a very sultry night, which, with the mosquitos, made the room almost unbearable. Added to this, our room led into a passage, so that anything like privacy was impossible. Our luggage did not arrive till nearly midnight, and then I found my box had been left at the depôt, so I could not get a change of clothes. A bath, however, I did get, but it was of a most primitive kind, and I had to go outside to get to it. It was very dirty, as indeed was the whole place, and I nearly used the small supply of water up in cleansing the bath. There were mosquitos here also, and, what is infinitely worse, bugs abounded, so I got very little rest.

We rose early next morning, and Mr. Bronson came to see us and gave us the pleasing intelligence that we could not possibly carry out the object of our journey, namely, to visit a cattle range on the Pecos River, as all his men were away rounding-up, and no outfit could be got. Personally, I was not very sorry, as I rather dreaded the long drive in the sun, and we should have been away at least three days and nights roughing it most uncomfortably. Mr. Bronson came to call on me, and we all lunched together in the coffee room of the hotel. The fare provided was bad, but as it included iced tea and ices we did not complain, and after luncheon we drove to the Old Mission House, built in 1617—quite an ancient edifice for this new world. It was merely a plain good sized chapel, with a rough altar and two places for confession, white-washed and paved; but, oh, so deliciously cool. The drive to it was through a large wood of pepper trees—graceful, shrubby trees, not large. We drove in a sort of Berlin with a movable top. J—— and Mr. B—— went in a light four-wheeled buggy, and I rather envied them. After "doing" the Mission House thoroughly we drove on by the Forts and over a very hilly and much-wooded country to see the source of the San Antonio River. Such a pretty spot. A tiny deep bubbling pool surrounded by trees in full leaf, and the ground covered with bright green grass and wild flowers. It seemed almost impossible that such a broad river could rise out of so small a spring and so quickly as it does.

San Antonio has nothing to recommend it, as it is not picturesquely old and ugly, or modernly clean and comfortable. It is sufficiently wild and savage to make it quite unsafe to be out and about after dusk, as the Mexicans abound, and they are far more dangerous than the Indians. There are two huge stores here, where one can buy anything. I got a good sombrero, and J—— a big Mexican hat. We also laid in a small store of fruit, bread, and hard boiled eggs for our journey to Los Angelos, as there are no breakfast or dining places for thirty-six hours of the journey. We also took a demijohn of light claret, and I made some cold tea.

I think our second night at Manenk's was worse than the first; even the inhabitants were astonished at the excessive heat, which resolved itself into thunder, and a fearful storm raged when we left at 6:40 p.m. on Saturday the 14th. We had more trouble about our checks than ever, as our passes carried us on from El Paso, and the official could not or would not be made to see this. However, at the very last moment, he handed J—— the tickets and we started in blissful ignorance of what the future had in store for us. I must mention that we had anxiously expected our letters at San Antonio, but as none came J—— went off to the office to make a last inquiry. "Oh yes," he was told, "a big packet had been sent by the boy at the same time as a telegram an hour before." Now the telegram had been left, but that horrid boy had forgotten the letters, and as neither he nor they were to be found, we were obliged to start in the sad state of uncertainty as to whether

21

we should ever get them; and those only who know by experience how precious to the traveller are the home letters can appreciate the bitter disappointment we felt. As before, the drawing room car was close and stuffy, and no washing apparatus was provided; our bags and rugs nearly filled up the vacant space, and I think we all felt rather out of heart at the prospect of three days and nights to be spent in such wretched quarters. However, we settled ourselves as well as we could, and after a very light supper of sandwiches and cold tea we all turned in. Curiously enough the night was bitterly cold, and we were glad of all our wraps; my fur cloak was a real comfort to me.

The country through which we passed was in a very unsettled state, as the Apaches were on the "war path." A band of them had harried a small village through which we passed, and driven off the horses and cattle. General Cook was in hot pursuit of them. All the officials of our train were fully armed, for although the Indians never have attacked a train, or thought of trying to upset one, yet there is always the possibility of their doing so. It was, therefore, rather a trial to one's nerves to be roused up in the middle of the night by a mighty jolt, and to hear screams in the night car. In a few moments the train pulled up; our party were up and out at once, as were the conductors, porters, &c., and lights gleamed outside. The cause of the jolt which had so nearly wrecked us was soon discovered, as the carcase of an ox was found across the line, where it had evidently been placed by some evil-minded persons. How the cow catcher had missed throwing it off no one could explain; anyway it was a lucky escape, and we all felt very thankful that the cruel design had been frustrated. Some people inclined to the belief that it was some private revenge on the part of a Mexican that had prompted it. The Mexicans are a brutal and treacherous people, and are much more to be dreaded than the Indians.

We had no cause to complain of cold after the first night, as the heat became oppressive. The country through which we passed was singularly uninteresting, as it was mostly vast sandy tracts, stretching as far as the eye could see. Nothing to break the monotony but giant cactus, ten or twelve feet high, and as thick as a man's body, which grew in groups, stretching out their thick stunted arms as if in despair. In the dusk they had a very weird, spectre-like appearance.

We saw the junction of the Rio Grande and the Pecos the second morning of our journey, and that was the last glimpse at anything like vegetation for some time. Our provisions turned out very badly. The bread and cold meat dried up so hard that we could not bite it, and my cold tea turned sour; so we had to eat our eggs and oranges and drink claret. I never dreamt how really essential a piece of bread is to one's comfort before.

We passed through Arizona and entered New Mexico without perceiving much change of country. We managed to get a little breakfast at a place called Deming, which revived us all. The stations along this comparatively new line to Sanderson city consisted of a couple of wooden huts, and at one place —where J—— got out to send a wire—of three old railway cars, one of which was fitted up as a telegraph office. We passed Yuma, on the Colorado river, at 3:30 a.m. I mention this place because it is 300 feet below the level of the sea, and the heat and dust were terrible; I

23

hardly thought we could endure it for another twelve hours. We stopped for dinner at some place the name of which I forget, but I was past eating then, as my head ached frightfully from the constant rattle of the cars, which becomes a positive torture after a little while. I asked the woman who was mistress of the dining saloon if I might have a cup of coffee sent out to me, as I was too ill to face the heat of the room. She coolly told me if I could not do as the rest did I must go without.

Words cannot tell how thankful I was when we left the sandy deserts and came into a green and watered country. My first glimpse of California was enchanting after the hot dreary journey across the sandy plains. It was almost as good as a bath to look at the deep rivers fringed with green trees and covered with flocks of waterfowl. Presently we were in fairyland truly, as the train passed the orchards of splendid orange groves, the oranges piled in great heaps, or weighing down the trees nearly to the ground.

It was nearly seven o'clock on Tuesday evening when we stopped at the queer Los Angelos station. There are no buildings except a depôt for goods and a ticket office, and the train pulls up at a sort of level crossing and goes through the town more in the fashion of a tramcar than of a railway. At the station there were three large old-fashioned coaches, each belonging to its special hotel. We had been recommended to stop at the Cosmopolitan, and drove there accordingly. It certainly was a vast improvement on Manenk's, and I got a bed room opening into a verandah, cool and airy, if not as clean as one could wish. Naturally we were all longing for a bath and change of raiment; but no luggage was forthcoming, and now we learned the sad fact that, after all the trouble about it at San Antonio, we had been done, as our checks were only made out to El Paso, and at that place all our boxes were stranded. It was a cruel blow, as there was not a chance of our getting them for at least three days, as so many stupid formalities had to be gone through before the railway authorities would give them up. Eventually J—— and I sallied out and got what was most essential at a sort of slop shop, and after a delicious bath and a very indifferent supper we all felt more inclined to take a cheerful view of things; at first I fear our angry passions did rise, and I still think it was too bad. Needless to say, this *contretemps* left us more in favour of our English railway arrangements than ever.

We much enjoyed our enforced stay at Los Angelos, as it gave us an opportunity of visiting the country in its vicinity. It is a very pretty spot. The Sierra Madre range of mountains bound one side, and the remainder seems to slope away in endless green hills and valleys, all covered with fruit trees and vineyards; but, though beautiful to look at, the oranges are very inferior to the Florida, being thick skinned and juiceless. We made an expedition to the Sierra Madre Villa, a charming hotel some thirteen miles from Los Angelos, situated quite at the foot of the hills in really charming Italian-like scenery. The garden was a blaze of geraniums, roses, heliotrope and sweet pinks; and, although the oranges were quite ripe, the air was sweet with the scent of the bloom as well. We drove through Mr. Rose's vineyards. He is the largest grape grower in these parts, and this year he had sold his oranges on the trees for a very large sum. We were told he is the largest wine grower in the world, and certainly his vineyards seemed endless. There are numbers of grizzly bears in the Sierras, and our driver, a talkative Mexican, told us many anecdotes of their predatory habits. They seem very fond of honey, and will go any distance to where hives are kept. These they overturn and then proceed to eat the honey, beating down the bees, and treading on them, "for all the world like a man," as he described it. Not very long ago it was the great sport and delight of Los Angelos to trap a grizzly and carry him off a prisoner, to be fastened to a ring in a kind of court erected for the purpose, and then drive in to him a savage bull. The animals were forced to fight, and the bull invariably got the worst of it, the bear tearing out his tongue when he opened his mouth to bellow, and so ended the horrid sight. After two or three bulls had been destroyed, the bear was shot. I am glad to say this brutal sport is now illegal, but the driver did not seem to share my feelings at all on the subject, and regretted the old free days very much.

Pepper trees seem to grow everywhere about Los Angelos. These trees are very pretty, with their feathery foliage and bright red berries. During my country walks I made quite a collection of wild flowers, some of them extremely pretty. Land has risen greatly in this part of California during the last few years, and whereas but ten years ago any one could have settled on a plot for a nominal sum, it is impossible now to purchase any, except at most exorbitant rates. As soon as the Californians master the art of wine making, and find out what vines really are the best for the soil, it will go hard with the Spanish and French wine growers. So far the phylloxera is unknown in California.

The country houses are charmingly built, with pretty gardens and verandahs, covered with lovely creepers. The place reminded me of Mauritius, only that, instead of the deadly close climate there, here it was brisk and bright—almost chilly. The summers are very hot, they say, but the nights are always cool. As to the town itself, I cannot say much in its praise; it is a straggling, ugly place, with wide, unpaved streets, and double lines for steam cars. There are some very good shops; better, indeed, than in New York, and the contents are not nearly so dear. There is a theatre, which, however, we did not visit; a post office, at which we frequently called, but always in vain (our letters here again having somehow gone wrong); and bars and saloons without number. The hotels are very bad, and extremely expensive. Of course we lived at the *table d'hôte*, as private rooms are quite unheard of in America. Visitors dine, breakfast, and sup together, and congregate afterwards in the public rooms. I found out our English plan of separate living rooms is voted very dull; and they dislike our English hotels very much, on account of their lack of public sitting rooms. The food of the Cosmopolitan was very bad and scanty. It was quite a case of first come first served; but the waiters were civil and obliging. The evenings were quite chilly, and it rained all one day, and the streets were at once converted into mud baths.

We made up our mind to leave on Friday evening, luggage or no luggage, and great was our joy to find that it was in the train that we had settled to go on to Madera by. J—— and Mr. B—— travelled in the van with it, and managed to change their light clothes for rough and warm garments. As we were now on our

27

way to the world-renowned Yosemite Valley we expected to find snow and frost there. I, alas! could not follow their example, but they managed to unearth my warm jacket and thick gloves.

Our journey from Los Angelos to Madera ought only to have taken eight hours, but owing to a hurricane that caught us shortly after entering the Mohave desert we were delayed five hours. Such a storm I never remember anywhere, either on sea or land. Our train was brought to a stand, and such was the violence of the gale that the heavy Pullman cars positively rocked like cradles. The noise was deafening, and showers of sand were dashed against the windows. The turntable could not be used it was so clogged with sand, and the second engine could not be got out until after quite four hours passed in this unpleasant manner. At length the wind abated and presently sank to rest, leaving us to continue our way in peace. We were then climbing over the mountain on an almost perpendicular line. On gaining the top the descent is almost as rapid, and two months before our visit a fearful accident had occurred. The train had reached the summit and the second engine had been taken off; the conductor and brakesman had got down, but the latter had neglected to put on his brake; something—no one knew what—started the carriages, and they began to move down the incline, at first so slowly that had either of the men had the presence of mind to jump on and put on one of the brakes, there seems to be no doubt that it would have been sufficient to avert the fearful calamity. They made no effort, however, and on rushed the train. The couplings miraculously broke just before coming to a siding, and all but one doomed Pullman car rattled down the siding, and beyond a severe jolting

when brought up, escaped further injury. Owing to
the furious speed the remaining car leaped and jolted
to such an extent that the lamps got thrown out of
their sockets and fell, deluging everything with
petroleum. Of course, as is always the practice, both
doors of the sleeping car were locked, and the
unhappy inmates were burnt to cinders almost in
sight of some few more fortunate passengers who,
owing to the crowded state of the train, were passing
the night in the smoking saloon, and so escaped a
miserable death. The story was told me by one of the
survivors, with numerous pathetic details which I
can never easily forget.

Quite five hours late the little station of Madera
was reached, and we hurried out to see if the stage
had awaited our arrival. Of course it had started, but
as we were a party of five, the stage proprietor agreed
to send us on in a light covered kind of Berlin as far as
Clerk's Hotel, some sixty-six miles on our way, and
though we found ourselves terribly cramped, and did
not care for our travelling companions, a Philadel-
phian bride and bridegroom, with the harshest
voices and most prominent nasal twang I have ever
heard, our anxiety to get into the romantic precincts
of the Yosemite would not allow of our waiting till
next day, so we pushed ourselves in as well as we
could and started.

It was a lovely drive after we had passed the long
dreary flat country that runs some twelve miles out,
and we soon came amongst the rocks and trees, the
beginning of the vast forest of pines through which
our road chiefly led us. The early spring was just
beginning to break, and the ground was covered for
miles with flowers of every hue, the commonest kinds
being the lovely blue and white nemophila. We had

never seen anything so delightful as the masses of these delicate flowers interspersed with others whose names I do not know, but often meet with in old-fashioned gardens given to the production of annuals. Here in these wilds they spring up yearly, an ever-increasing crop.

The roads were so heavy that we found it impossible to do the journey to Clerk's Hotel in one day, so we halted for the night at Coarse Gold Gulch, where there was a quaint wooden house belonging to a German family. The stages usually stopped here to enable their passengers to dine, but people very seldom stayed the night. The accommodation was simple in the extreme, as may be expected, and not too clean; still we did get separate bed rooms and beds to sleep on. It was lovely weather; in the middle of the day the heat was great, but the evening was delicious, and we sat under the verandah till quite late. After a plentiful breakfast we started again next morning, feeling quite fresh and invigorated by the lovely mountain air. I started ahead of the trap, and walked on some way. It was lovely all alone in the forest. Hundreds of little grey squirrels ran about at my feet; unlike the squirrels at home, these live in holes in the ground. The tapping of the industrious woodpecker sounded on all sides, and lovely plumaged birds flew up into the trees at my approach; my presence did not appear to much disturb them. Words would fail me to describe all the pretty sights and sounds we met with on our lonely forest drive. We toiled on over the most primitive roads, the scenery becoming wilder and more dreary, till, just as night was falling, we reached our welcome hotel, very weary and almost shaken to pieces. However, a delicious bath (an unwonted luxury in these out-of-the-way regions) and a really well-cooked and neatly served dinner soon restored our energies, and we rushed off directly our repast was over to see the sun set and the waterfalls. We were rewarded for a rough walk by the sweetest Welsh scenery imaginable, very like the Precipice Walk at Hengwart, only, of course, on a much larger scale.

Next morning we took our seats in the stage, a description of *char-à-banc* for four sets of passengers and drawn by six horses. If I had found our journey of the previous day a rough one, I soon discovered it was as nothing compared to this. We went at score down the hills, utterly regardless of deep ruts, branches of fallen trees, and stones. Our driver, with a grim sense of humour, would exclaim on nearing some awful chasm, "Here we go!" and go we certainly did, our heads almost going through the covering with which the vehicle was provided to keep off the sun. At the earliest opportunity many of us left the stage when it stopped to change horses and hastened on ahead. So heavy was the road at times, and so difficult for six horses to drag the coach up the steep inclines, that I was able to walk quite seven miles before the vehicle overtook me, a feat which elicited much astonishment from our Jehu, as the true American never walks unless really compelled; but for a woman to make use of her limbs in such a manner was indeed unheard of.

We lunched by a charming stream; quite a picnic it was, the luncheon having been sent from Clerk's Hotel. We made the acquaintance of some Australians, just landed, who were on their way home, and also of a Mr. C——, a very pleasant young American,

educated in England, and very English in his ways.
We became great friends, and met him more than
once after leaving the Yosemite.

I think the view from Inspiration Point, looking
down into the valley, is quite the most impressive in
the world; it is glorious; but description is impossible.
I would only say to my reader, "See it for yourself,
only go a month later than we did, take your own
outfit, allow yourself plenty of time to do the journey
and so make it a delightful expedition, instead of, as
in our case, a very painful and intensely disagreeable
one." Truly, the journey in and out by public stage is
so hateful that one feels to have paid too dearly for
the wonderful and soul-awing scenery that greeted
us at the end; and the society of vulgar fellow-
travellers destroys the romance entirely. We could
not get away from them; they seemed to pursue us
everywhere.

El Capiten is certainly the king of the rocks. It
stands 3,300 feet above the valley at its entrance to
the left, and appears as if hewn out of the mountain.
It presents a perfectly smooth surface. I do not,
however, purpose describing all the wonders of this
wondrous valley, as the guide books do so better than
I could. I will merely say that, to my mind, the Bridal
Veil Falls—called Pohona, "Spirit of the Evil Wind,"
by the Indians—which falls over the cliff on the west
side of the Cathedral Rock, a fall of 900 feet; the
Vernal Falls, which is a cataract of 600 feet, and is
more picturesque, but not so perpendicular; and the
view from Glacier Point, are certainly the most
striking features. The Mirror Lake is a fraud, as it is
merely a duck pond, and the phenomenon of seeing
the sun rise in its depths can be seen equally well on
any perfectly placid sheet of water at home or abroad.

There are many excursions to be made in the
valley, and in the month of June a week might be
well spent there. We were too early for the spring
flowers, and the trees were only beginning to bud;
indeed, the snow lay so deep on the mountain paths
that it was hardly safe to attempt them, and going up
to Glacier Point a sad accident befell us, which quite
spoilt my pleasure in the expedition. We started a
party of six on horse and mule back. Mr. B——
preferred to walk the whole way, and got to the top
some time ahead of us. It was a narrow, winding, and
almost perpendicular path, and the snow got so hard
and slippery before we were half way up that, warned
by an ominous stumble or two of my little grey mare,
I insisted on dismounting, and J—— and I scrambled
up on foot the rest of the way. One of the party, a
heavy, unwieldy Australian, insisted upon his
"pound of flesh," and as he had paid for a horse ride he
would have it. The guide exchanged his own pony—a
very strong, young one—for the Leviathan's mule,
warning him not to touch the bridle, as it was one of
the cruel Mexican bits—horrible instruments of
torture. After proceeding a few yards the guide's
horse slipped over some rough ice and nearly fell; of
course, the rider tugged furiously at the bridle, and
the horse on recovering itself reared on end. The
Australian had just time to slip off before the poor
creature, losing its foothold, plunged over the edge of
the precipice, and disappeared for ever, carrying
with it the guide's outfit, together with Mr. B——'s
irreplaceable ulster, which I had advised him to give
the guide at starting. So thin was the ice near the
precipice that it was found quite impossible to get
anywhere near where the poor horse was; the saddle
and blanket were seen lying half way down, but no

trace of the horse was ever found. Poor beast! how I hope he was dead ere he reached the bottom. As you can imagine, this cast a gloom over us all, and after doing "the point," and getting most thoroughly wet through in a damp soft drizzle, we turned and walked to the bottom much faster than we had ridden up.

Not a word of the accident was allowed to find its way into the papers. We were told that accidents of this kind were not uncommon, and that the last victim was a lady, who fell with her horse, and was so much injured that she died shortly after being rescued. Great care is taken not to give publicity to such matters, lest the public should take fright.

The hotels are very bad at present; we stayed at Cook's, but I do not think this is the best. Anyway, I must warn anyone who may visit these parts to beware what they say when in their bed rooms. The walls are merely lath and paper, and we overheard a funny conversation between a Pennsylvanian bride and bridegroom, who were next but one to us, that was certainly not intended to be public property; and as listeners proverbially hear no good of themselves, our experience was no better than the average, as the "darned stuck-up Britishers" came in for a good share of this couple's abuse. It was, however, very amusing, and though I tried to make them aware of the situation by coughing, throwing things on the ground, &c., it was of no avail, and, tired though I was, I could get no sleep till past midnight.

We only spent two days in the valley, as time was precious, and then retraced our steps back to Clerk's. To give my readers an idea of the state of the roads I may mention that it was twenty-eight miles from the Yosemite to Clerk's, and it took us eight and three-quarter hours to do it. We had six horses and

changed twice. Of course we were bound to visit the
"Big Trees," or Marriposa Grove, so after a hasty
lunch we set off in a light brake. The snow came down
heavily, and spoiled the view considerably; but the
trees are certainly wonderful. They do not, however,
stand together in a grove; we came upon them one by
one, and the effect is not so surprising. As the pines
are so very large the sight of one larger than the rest
does not astonish one. They are sadly burnt and
scorched at the base by the Indians; the height of the
tallest is over two hundred and seventy feet, and the
circumference at the ground eighty-nine feet. One
tree, much burnt, is more than one hundred feet in
circumference, and we actually drove our team and
brake through the divided roots of one of the giants.
They are chiefly red wood pine, but the Californian
sugar pine grows to an immense height, and is more
graceful and symmetrical Altogether, in spite of
many drawbacks and the terrible fatigue and
suffering we endured from the jolting of our
conveyance, it was a very delightful expedition, and
left an undying remembrance.

We slept at Clerk's that night, and then pushed on
by train to Madera, a dreadful place, where we got
some supper—at least, tried to get some, but the
swarms of black flies made this an almost hopeless
task. We then had our beds made up in the sleeping
railway car, and, fortunately, were the only passengers, so enjoyed a really delightful rest, and at
about three in the morning the Southern train came
up and whirled us away *en route* for San Francisco.

We had quite jumped into spring at last. The sun
was delightfully warm, but not hot, and anything
more brilliant than the flowers along the railway
banks I have never seen, masses of gorgeous colours,

yellow and blue predominating. It was about midday
when we reached Oatlands. This is *the* suburb of San
Francisco, and lies upon the opposite side of the bay
to the metropolis. It is seven miles across. An
excellent steamer meets the trains, and takes the
passengers, bag and baggage, to the Sixteenth-street
Station. As usual, there were no porters, although
Oatlands is a very large station, so we had to struggle
with our luggage as best we could through a jostling
crowd, and were all shut into a big waiting room.
After some twenty minutes of discomfort the doors
were thrown open, and we were fairly swept along in
the crowd on board. Our luggage was left to its fate;
but on this occasion it came on all right.

The landing at "Frisco" was even worse than the
getting on board, as a crowd of idlers, hotel touts, and
ruffians of every kind were awaiting us, and I was
nearly torn to pieces amongst them. However, we
secured a crazy kind of fly, drawn by two horses, and
were soon safely installed at the Palace Hotel. I
suppose this is really the largest hotel in the world. It
is a huge building, has been twice burnt down, and is
now supposed to be fireproof. You enter into a large
courtyard, somewhat like the Grand Hotel in Paris,
and after an interview with Mr. Smith at the office,
we were conducted to the lift, and presently found
ourselves on the fifth floor in quite the most
comfortably furnished rooms we had seen since we
left home. The rooms are really charming, airy,
large, and fitted with every convenience, even
writing tables and a nice marble bath, with hot and
cold water, to every suite. As our luggage actually
arrived within an hour after we got in we were able to
indulge in a complete change of raiment, a luxury we
had been forced to dispense with for ten days. The

intense enjoyment of a bath under these circumstances can only be understood by those who, like ourselves, had been so long deprived of the comfort. I was too tired to do any sightseeing, and as all our letters had at last reached us, the delight of reading them and beginning my answers took up the rest of the afternoon and evening. We dined at the *table d'hôte*, and found the cooking very fair, but the attendance, as usual, very bad.

We were greatly disappointed with "Frisco," having heard it so extravagantly praised. It is a big town, with wide but dirty streets. It is built up a very steep hill-side, and certainly looks very picturesque from the bay. Cable tramcars are used up these steep ascents; they look very uncanny, running up so noiselessly and apparently of their own free will. The Chinamen are greatly astonished by them, and cannot make it out at all. "No pullee, no pushee, go up hilly like helly." Of course, I went up in them, and they are very pleasant—so smooth and noiseless. There is a large park belonging to the city, which is by no means well cared for at present. We drove through it on our way to the Cliff House to see the sea lions—such huge beasts, lying all about the rocks in hundreds, and it was most interesting to watch them. Some romped about like children bathing, jumping off the rocks into the sea and swimming round to land again, and then re-plunging in pursuit of one another. Sometimes a real battle takes place between two old veterans, and their cries sound strange and fierce through the serf. The sea all about was dotted with multitudes of round heads swimming and fishing. There is a law forbidding the sea lions being molested or destroyed. They really swarm to such an extent that the fishermen complain

37

greatly of the damage they do to their trade. There was some talk of a petition to reduce their numbers. It is rather curious that nearly all the fishermen are Italians. They look very picturesque in their native garb.

We made a charming expedition to the Geysers at Calistoga, a day's journey from San Francisco. We left by ferry-boat for Cloverdale at seven o'clock on a lovely morning. The Golden Gate really deserves its name, and the bay is like a sheet of glass. Arrived at Cloverdale, we took our seats in the stage, a very uncomfortable conveyance. It was a lovely drive through strange scenery. For the greater part of the journey we drove along the edge of sheer precipices, with no protection in the shape of fence or wall at all. Then we entered some lovely forests; the trees were here in full leaf. By-and-bye a huge cloud of steam in the distance indicated we were nearing the sulphur springs. I think the distance was some sixty-three miles altogether, and we took nearly eleven hours to do it, arriving at the pretty little hotel, so like a Swiss chalet, at a little after half-past five. We were received and welcomed by the landlady, an English-woman, in the most hospitable fashion. She is well known as the most attentive, civil, and kind hostess in California, and it was such a pleasure to see her bright kind face and hear her cheery voice; so different to the usual sour indifference travellers meet with at the hotels. After a cup of excellent tea we started off to climb the hill to the burning springs.

A party under the charge of a guide were just in front of us, and wanted us to go with them, but we could not endure their slow crawl, and soon left them behind. The ground got very hot, and it was fortunate we had prepared ourselves for the sulphur by putting on our oldest boots and clothes, as everything we wore got more or less injured by the fumes. The poor ladies whom we left toiling up in their black silk dresses and thin shoes were loud in their complaints on their return.

The springs themselves are not worth going to see, as they do not rise in jets at all, but only in steam, with the single exception of one, called "The Devil's Punch Bowl," which bubbles up with great noise and inward groaning. The scenery of the whole place is charming; I saw nothing that pleased me more, and should have dearly liked to stay a few days to explore the hills and vales.

On our return, we found a very simple, but excellent supper awaiting us, to which we did full justice, and then sauntered out in the gardens and fed the monkey, who was an ill-tempered brute, with no manners. Shortly after sunset it became very dull, and we were glad to get indoors and sit by the fire till bed-time. We were up very early next morning in order to have a good look at the Geysers. They were steaming away as if they meant to blow up, but subsided after the sun rose. "Young Foss" was to have been our driver on this occasion, but, owing to an unpleasant misunderstanding, I had to "stand down," and take my place in a smaller vehicle, drawn by a pair of beautiful chesnuts. Our driver was an elderly man, and was very civil to me. He knew everything connected with the country, told me wonderful yarns about bears, mad skunks, and a solitary Frenchman, who had settled in this lovely but lonely part of the world twenty years before, and who never saw a soul to speak to, except our driver and a few hunters who lived in the neighbourhood. He also stopped to let me gather some pretty flowers and curious ferns; and, in short, made the drive extremely pleasant for me. "Young Foss" is the son of the very celebrated driver, of whom so many stories are told, and who is considered quite the best whip out West, and of whom more anon. Before we started J—— took a sulphur bath, and declared it had a marvellously refreshing effect. It had a horrid smell, though, and not at all an inviting appearance; but many people stay here for weeks on purpose to take the baths, which are voted excellent by the faculty for many complaints, and more particularly for rheumatism.

I was really sorry when we reached Pine Flat, as there another stage met us and we gave up our pony carriage and pleasant driver. We had distanced Young Foss's heavy conveyance, so had time to explore a little and to make a few purchases of California diamonds, sticks cut from the forest, &c., and for me to gather some lovely wild flowers. A few years back Pine Flat had a population of 2,000 inhabitants, fine houses were built, a post office erected, and everything flourished. When we stopped there there were five men and one woman living in the desolate spot; the few houses that remained were in ruins, the rest were all burnt down. It was the quicksilver mines that had set it up for a short spell, and then as suddenly brought it down. Quicksilver fell from 1 dollar 60 cents an ounce to 30 cents, so, of course, the concern burst up and the miners departed as quickly as they had assembled.

Our drive was certainly most lovely the whole way from the Sulphur Canon to Foss's Hotel, and for the greater part, once we were out of the hilly district, through park-like land. I never saw such splendid grass; it grows knee-deep everywhere. Habitations of

any kind were few and far between. Part of the road
was most precipitous, and so winding that we often
lost sight of our leaders round the sharp curves. We
had six horses in our team all the way, and the
perfect manner in which they were driven charmed
me greatly—so quietly and easily, though we were
going at a hand gallop. Certainly, they can drive in
California; and it was a difficult and dangerous road.
We had a capital luncheon at Foss's Hotel, and then
we made the acquaintance of the veritable driver so
often mentioned by Bret Harte in "Roughing It." He
was a most arbitrary landlord, and inclined to be
very disagreeable, chiefly, I think, because we none
of us cared to drive some nine miles to see the
remains of the petrified forest. We had been
previously warned not to go, as this so-called forest is
nothing but a few old logs lying about here and there.
However, after bullying two very quiet and inof-
fensive Germans he got better, and even proposed to
drive our party on to Calistoga with his own
particular pair of little mustangs. Such wonderful
little beasts: they were not over 13 hands, and took
along our brake, with eight people and baggage—not
to speak of Mr. Foss himself, who certainly weighed
near 18 stone—as if it were a very ordinary load;
indeed, for the first few miles it took all he knew to
hold them. He was very pleased at my admiration for
them, and said he always found his lady passengers
took interest in the horses, whereas most of the men
did not know a good horse from a bad; and he
proceeded to tell me an anecdote, which I must
repeat, as it shows so well what can be done in a
"free" country, where might is right.

Foss was driving his team with a fair load from
Calistoga to Pine Flats, and on changing horses for

the second time, one of his passengers, a lady of course, began to talk to him about his horses, and to praise their sagacity, as they seemed to understand all he said, and not to require any guidance at all. A man who was seated behind made some slighting remark upon the feminine folly that could believe in the sagacity of a horse—a brute only intended to drag a stage or carry its load, as it was made to go; and he continued talking in this strain till Foss, who was walking his team up a steep hill, reached the top. He pulled up, and turning to the man, bade him get down; not knowing what for, the man did as he was told, when Foss quietly handed him his bag and the money he had paid for his fare, and merely observing that "anyway he did not intend to carry such cattle with his horses," drove on and left the unfortunate to his fate. He had at least ten miles to walk before he would reach the place where the horses were changed, and he could get no redress, as Foss was "boss" of the road.

We reached Calistoga an hour before the train started, so, to while away the time, Foss showed us the town and then his stables and horses. The stables, built on his own plan, were really good, and the horses seemed well cared for and were quite friendly.

We arrived at the station just in time to catch the train, and after a friendly parting with the worthy Foss started on our return to Frisco, which we reached in time for supper. We had all greatly enjoyed the trip.

Soon after this the weather changed very much for the worse—sea fogs and heavy rain—so we resolved to leave San Francisco, and run down to the

far-famed Monterey, the queen of American watering-places. It is 125 miles from San Francisco, and
the express—a "daisy" train, as it is called—does the
journey in three and a-half hours—the fastest going
on the Pacific coast, as there are ten stoppages,
including dinner at Gilroy. We were to have stopped
at ex-Governor Stanfield's horse farm on the way,
but the weather was too bad. The scenery going down
was not particularly pretty, but Monterey, or rather
the Hotel del Monte, is a lovely place, and quite the
best of American hotels. It was built in 1880, about a
mile from the little village. The site selected was in a
grove of pine, oak and cedar, the trees being
sufficiently scattered to admit of drives, footpaths,
lawns, and beds of lovely flowers. One hundred and
twenty acres were set aside and enclosed as hotel
grounds, and seven thousand more were purchased
for other purposes, such as drives and rides. The
hotel is built in the Modern Gothic style, and cost
altogether a quarter of a million dollars. The bed
rooms are very large and airy, and very nicely
furnished. The public rooms are large and splendid,
and every sort of amusement—billiards, quoits,
bowling alley, &c.—duly provided. There is also good
stabling for sixty horses. All persons employed in the
gardens, excepting the head gardeners, were, I
think, Chinamen, and the flowers certainly did them
credit; they were very lovely. Many tame golden
pheasants were running about like poultry, and the
sweetest little squirrels swarmed up and down the
trees in the most impudent manner. The town of
Monterey, the former capital of California, is a poor,
dirty little place; it was founded by the Spaniards in
1602, and I should say it had not made much progress

since that time. It is really a noteworthy place in American history, and many quaint legends are told about the holy fathers and their converts. One of the oldest mission houses—the Carmel Mission, built by Father Junipero Serro—stands some few miles inland. Of course, it is now merely a ruin, but was well worth the scrambling drive we made to it across an almost impassable morass, which obliged us at last to leave the carriage and take to our feet. The scenery is supposed to resemble Italian, on account of the Monterey cypresses, which are very like the Italian stone pine. There is nothing at all remarkable about Monterey, except that it is very dirty. The one really curious feature of the place is the public bathing house, where any one can walk in and watch the antics of men and women bathing, romping, and swimming about together, utterly regardless of, to my English mind, the common decencies of life.

Our stay at Monterey had to be brief, and we returned to San Francisco very shortly, after bidding adieu to one of our party who remained there.

Having collected our luggage and received our letters, we started again at three in the afternoon for Lake Tahoe, *viâ* Truchi. At the station we found that all the seats in the sleeping car were taken, and though there were eight persons anxious to travel in one, the authorities rudely refused to allow another car to be attached. The train was crowded, and as there are on the American lines only the sleping cars and a kind of covered cattle truck they call the ordinary car—an infinitely dirtier and more uncomfortable conveyance than the worst style of third class carriage on our English lines—we were forced to crush into the latter, amongst about forty people—niggers, drunken men, and crying children. The floor

44

was so filthy that, having once got to my seat, I never stirred again till we reached Truchi at four o'clock next morning. This was quite the most dreadful night I ever spent, and as the seats are simply boarded and it is impossible to rest on them, I felt rather done up. However, it was a relief to get out and stretch our weary limbs. The little railway hotel is mentioned by Miss Bird as the place she started from on her mountain ride. The landlord told us all the beds were full, but some of the occupants, being miners, would be rising shortly, and I might lie down on the bed then. This kind offer I declined with thanks; and after a wretched breakfast of bad coffee and worse bread and butter, we started in the stage for Tahoe. I had the box seat, and got all the information I could from the driver, which certainly was not a great deal. The road was dreadful, as the snow lay deep in parts and the mud was over a foot deep; at places the passengers were compelled to alight, and they sunk up to their knees in the miry compound. The road ran through very wild, picturesque scenery—pine woods and hills on one side, and a swift running river below, down which were floating hundreds of tree trunks. In some places the river was choked by these impediments to its course, and it was a work of no small danger to the lumberer to climb over the floating mass with his long pole and to free them from their entanglement.

It was an eventful drive, and once or twice we were nearly over, as the stage was topheavy, but we managed to reach Tahoe about three in the afternoon. It is a lovely spot. The lake is about twenty-five miles long by fourteen wide, and is surrounded by snow-clad mountains and pine woods. There are two hotels here, but the best of the two was closed, as it was too early for visitors. The smaller one we put up at was kept by some Germans, and we found it fairly comfortable. We discovered that one of our bags had fallen off the stage somewhere, and we were in dispair at ever seeing it again, but fortunately a buggy coming behind us had found it, and brought it on.

It was such a lovely afternoon that we hired a boat and went out to try and catch some of the famous lake trout. The water of the lake is so clear we could see right down to a depth of thirty feet, and the air was delicious and invigorating. Altogether, we much enjoyed the row. The next day we went round the lake in the steamer and landed opposite at Glenbrook, where we had a capital luncheon off one of the trout, and then went on by stage to Carson City, some sixteen miles. J—— and I started to walk, as it was very steep, and here we came across what is called a "flume," used for carrying down the lumber. It is a narrow deep ledge cut all along the mountain side and running right down to the valley filled with water, and down this the logs race like lightning one after the other in endless succession. It made me dizzy to watch them. Where the "flume" bends abruptly, men are posted to help the logs on their monotonous way. I was told that a lad once got astride a log and shot down till he was stopped by a bend; he never got over it, as he became a hopeless cripple. Carson City is a very desolate place, standing on a wide plain covered with scrub and very little cultivation. Here we rejoined the train, and here I saw a number of the Digger Indians, a miserable race, small and wretched-looking, but with a strong Irish cast of face—quite the lowest Irish type. These Digger Indians eat roots, insects, grubs, and in fact almost anything. Though they do not work, yet to beg they are not ashamed. They are, indeed, a disgusting race. We went on by train to Reno, and stayed at the Depôt Hotel, where we obtained a fair supper and comfortable beds.

Next morning, about seven o'clock, we started again for Salt Lake City. It was a weary journey through the desert, and was very hot and dusty. The train barely went fifteen miles an hour and the shaking was terrific. I could not read even, and to write was impossible. We stopped twice to partake of food, but of course the fare provided was most miserable. There was no scenery to make the ride at all enjoyable, and I was extremely glad to reach Ogden the following morning, where we changed trains, and succeeded in getting some fairly good coffee. The climate was so different to California; a hot, dry air filled with sand—even the wind was hot. We passed the dead lake, where if anything is left in the water for some time it comes out white with alkali. Not a fish lives in, or a waterfowl upon, its waters, and all around is white as a frost.

Salt Lake City very much disappointed us. No doubt it is a marvel of industry, and the wonderful way the Mormons have cultivated these arid plains, and made blooming orchards and gardens where formerly was only rock and scrub, is highly commendable, while the city boasts some good public buildings and houses and some large shops; but we had heard so much of its beauty and scenery, and both these we certainly found conspicuous by their absence. The tabernacle is curious—a huge beehive, capable of holding some thousands of worshippers. The Mormons' emblem is a beehive; they have it over their co-operative store—a huge shop kept entirely by Mormons—and there I immediately went, ostensibly to buy a print dress, in reality to talk with the shop people, and try to learn something about them and their ways; but I found them very reticent, and they indignantly resent the advent of "Gentiles." Of course they do not allow that they practise polygamy at all now; but all the same, there are very few Mormon men who have not at least three wives.

We drove out to Jackson's Camp, where the soldiers are located, and then to see the principal elders' houses. All the streets are planted with fruit trees, and are irrigated by a small stream, which courses down one side; but as everything is emptied from the houses into this stream, it is quite the reverse of clear, and in some places was very nasty indeed. The hotel we stopped at was kept by a Gentile, who was, of course, very communicative about the Mormons and their, as he said, evil ways. He related numerous stories of their wickedness, which we listened to, but reserved the right to believe as much of as we pleased. It was a shockingly bad hotel; dirty and uncomfortable in the extreme. We attended service in the tabernacle, and saw some three thousand Mormons of both sexes assembled— the women weary, aged, toil-worn hags, not a single fresh, or young, or even happy face amongst them; the men all with a hard, determined stamp of face, just as one pictures the old Covenanters in Scott's novels; the elders, sleek, smug-looking individuals, evidently living well at the expense of their disciples.

It was a sacrament day, and eight elders, on the raised daïs which served as a pulpit and is also used for the preachers at one end, were tearing up bread into little bits and filling basins with the crumbs, much as a kitchenmaid shells peas. These basins were handed round, and everyone took some of the contents and munched it up. Then large flagons of water went round. I noticed one man take a good pull at this and then get it back from his neighbour and take another drink. And small wonder, for it was fearfully hot and stuffy, and no doubt the poor fellow was thirsty. We could not learn the name of the preacher; he was reputed one of their best speakers, and raved and ranted in truly orthodox fashion. The gist of his discourse went to prove that St. John the Evangelist's mantle had fallen on to the shoulders of Joe Smith, but after a short time he digressed to frantic abuse of the American Government. The discourse was long and noisy, and we left before he ended.

We were all glad to leave next day, and as rain had fallen during the night the distressing dust was laid. It was a lovely journey through Weber's Canon and Valley, with its rich grazing land and such wonderfully red sandstone hills of the quaintest shapes. We lunched at Ogden, and went on all night, reaching Cheyenne at midday not a bit tired, as there was so much to interest us all along the route.

Thus pleasantly ended what we may call, in the light of what was to follow, our journey through the "civilised" portion of the United States of America.

CHAPTER II

The Round-up

Aᴛᴇʀ nearly three months of continuous travelling, starting from New York, visiting Washington, St. Louis, on through dreary Arizona and fertile Texas, stopping at the quaint town of San Antonio long enough to see something of the country, then on to Los Angelos, most prosperous of Californian fruit-growing districts, and so into the wonders of the Yosemite Valley; halting for a brief interval at San Francisco and Monterey, visiting lovely Lake Tahoe, with its snowy horizon of blue mountains and its fir-clothed hills, which the lumberers' axe will, alas, soon destroy; introducing ourselves to the Mormons of Salt Lake City, and on through the wonderful scenery of Weber Canon and Valley; we at last reached our destination—Cheyenne City—at midday on the 15th May, 1883. An omnibus and pair met us from Dyer's Hotel, which considerate proceeding greatly surprised me, as I had been led to understand Cheyenne was still quite outside the pale of modern civilisation. However, I

found this a decided mistake, as, indeed, I had found
most of the information kindly bestowed upon us by
people who knew no more of the West than we did.
Dyer's was full, so we took up our abode at a big
square building with good sleeping accommodation,
a sitting room with a balcony and a piano, but with
the worst served and cooked *table d'hôte* we had met
with anywhere on our journey. However, Mr. R——
introduced the men of our party at the Cheyenne
Club, and there everything was very nice—in fact,
quite luxurious, after the "roughing" they had
undergone.

The weather was, if anything, a trifle too hot; so
much so, indeed, that I began to look rather with
dismay upon my thick homespun Norfolk suit, and to
contemplate getting a print dress, if such an article
could be obtained. Cheyenne was a much larger place
than I had imagined it would be, and not pretty by
any means: no trees or shrubs, very wide streets, and
some wonderfully good shops. I was able to get
several useful articles of ready made clothing,
including a chintz dressing gown, which replaced my
felt one—which had been spoiled by the Chinese
washing men—aprons, light shoes, a thick green
veil, the great comfort of which I found shortly, and
many other things I thought useful for our Prairie
expedition. One thing I could not get—a big white
umbrella or sunshade; such an article had never
been asked for before. Of course, the shopman who
supplied my wants put me through a thorough
examination. "I was English?" "How long had I been
in America?" "How did I like it?" "Guess it had
surprised me some?" "What was I doing in Cheyenne?" "Guess Englishwomen must be smart to

undertake to drive across the prairies!" "Guess he would not do it!" &c.

As I found it far better to humour the curiosity of those I had dealings with, I answered all inquiries pleasantly, and having paid for my purchases, and exchanged a hand shake across the counter, I next went in search of the "lady" who would be so obliging as to make up a print frock for me. I had proposed asking her to wait upon me, but was assured she would certainly not do that. After a long search, I found her house—a three-roomed cottage not far from our hotel; and on knocking, was told to walk right in. It reminded me so much of the story of the Sewing Bee in the "Wide Wide World."* Several women were seated all round the little room, working away and talking as if for their lives. My entrance caused no diversion, and I went up to one of the sewers and asked for Mrs. ———. "Guess I'm her," was the answer, with a strong nasal twang. While explaining my wants, one of the women got up and pushed a seat to me, for which courtesy I thanked her. Mrs. ——— was very civil, but in a manner which indicated perfect equality. She took an interest in my gown evidently, and suggested several modes, before I could persuade her that, as it was for very rough usage, the plainer and simpler the style the better. After this was settled, of course I had to explain my appearance in Cheyenne, our past travels, and future route. They all seemed vastly interested, especially to hear I had actually seen the Mormons. I had to invent some pressing engagement to make my escape, and was begged to come in again at an early date.

---

*[*The Wide, Wide World* (1851), by Susan Warner, was a very popular, moralistic story for girls.]

We only stayed a few days at Cheyenne, as we found it was quite too early to start for the Round-up. Snow had fallen lately, and the rivers were all out, and we decided to make a short trip by Denver City to Colorado to pass the time. Oh, how it rained the day we left Cheyenne! I never saw such rain. We got wet through between the omnibus and the cars, in spite of waterproofs and umbrellas. They kept us an hour at the station, and the car was filled with quite the dirtiest and roughest set I have yet travelled with. The train took us through the prairies for some distance, and we saw encamped by a stream a herd of cattle and their attendant cowboys, with the usual outfit. Such picturesque wild-looking fellows these cowboys were, in their wide-brimmed sombreros and leather chaps, all fringed, and wearing big Mexican spurs. But their horses disappointed me very much; poor thin rough little ponies, more like Welsh ponies than wild prairie horses; their heads hanging dejectedly as they stood disconsolately together in the pelting rain. I had heard so much of the wonderful riding of these same cowboys that I could not help asking, could these wretched ponies ever be difficult to manage?

I was pondering over this, when our train ran in to Denver Station about ten at night, and we had to bundle out in the torrents of rain, and make our way to the entrance, where several omnibuses were stationed. We had wired beforehand for rooms at The Windsor, and after about twenty minutes' severe jolting we stopped at a narrow entrance with a swing door. We pushed through this and entered a very dirty covered courtyard, with the enevitable "Bar" at the end. Having obtained the "key" of our rooms from the clerk, and a porter to carry our things, we mounted a long flight of stairs, and then went down a corridor carpeted with a thick handsome drugget; but the corridor was so overheated that it stifled us. At length we reached our rooms. Of course, my bed room opened out of a sitting room, an ingenious method much in vogue in these large hotels to extract a double "fare," as the sitting room is always charged extra. A coloured man brought up our luggage. Not a real darkey, but a half-caste, to my mind the most disagreeable race under the sun. Dinner was over, but we were in time for supper, which consisted of coffee, fish, and a variety of breads. They certainly do excel in America in the art of bread making. Such a variety, and all good. It was too late for me to go out, but J—— and Mr. B——, as the storm was over, strolled round. They found the streets so badly lighted and so muddy that they could not walk far.

Next morning it was fair, so after breakfast, which was served in another vast saloon, made red hot by means of stoves, we sallied forth to see the town. It is wonderful how quickly they build these places. A few years ago Denver was merely a mining village, consisting of a few movable huts. Since the railway came it is quite a large place. There is a very pretty opera house, a handsome post-office, and any number of stores. The streets are, of course, impassable in wet weather and are ankle-deep in mud. The lighting is very primitive; but no one seems to mind this in the Far West so long as the houses are built: the getting into them is the proprietor's concern. I nearly bought the dearest of green Mexican parrots, such a clever bird and so tame; but, alas! the owner put as high a value on it as a Parisian bird seller would, and we could not effect a deal. I got a tarantula's nest and some quaint Mexican pottery, and tried to obtain a white umbrella; but this last article was not to be had.

After luncheon we drove out to the Silver Smelting Works, and passed the afternoon watching the whole process. Very interesting it was, especially when, at the last, we were shown a row of solid shining silver bricks, about a foot in diameter, standing in a shed ready to be packed off. The manager kindly offered me one, on condition I was to carry it off. You will believe I tried my best, but I could not, it was so heavy. I thought he might have given me a little bit to keep as a curiosity, but this he did not offer. I, however, bought a curious little cross composed of eight different minerals, the product of the various mines about Denver. The fumes from the furnaces affected our eyes very much, and J—— suffered so much that he had to call on a doctor when he got to Colorado Springs. He turned out to be the same doctor who attended poor Clement Crossley, and who told him he ought not to have been sent out, as the climate only suited what they call chronic consumption and not those who are afflicted with acute consumption. The air is truly wonderfully rarefied. Every living creature feels it. A trotter that could do his mile at New York in three minutes with ease would require an extra allowance of time in Colorado. I found walking at all quickly decidedly more of an effort than I ever remember it; but this is not to be wondered at when we remember that we were 5,000 feet above the sea. The railway terminates at Manitou, and there, on a delicious evening, we got out. It had rained nearly ever since we left Cheyenne, but at Manitou it was a warm balmy rain that brought all the flowers and leaves bursting into bloom, and very pretty everything looked. Our hotel stood amongst trees, and looked across the valley towards the Garden of the Gods. Pike's Peak, on the other extremity, stands out in snowy relief from the dark pine forest that dots its feet.

Snow had fallen heavily a few days before, but only on the highest hills. I forget the name of our hotel, which is very ungrateful of me, as it was quite one of the nicest we had met with. We had wired for room, and found they had everything very nice for us, and even a fire in my bed room—a real luxury, and very unusual in this land of stoves. The dinner was excellent, and we afterwards wandered through the village for about a mile and a half, as far as a noted spring of mineral water. I delighted in the sweetness of the spring flowers, just beginning to peep out here and there.

We had made the acquaintance of a very pleasant English couple on their way home from China; we had been fellow travellers off and on for some time. They were very anxious to make the ascent of Pike's Peak the next morning, and begged us to go also. I did not really care about it. It looked so cold and so terribly high up, and I was not at all prepared for mountain climbing, having neither strong boots nor a rough dress with me. However, as all our party were quite inclined to go I gave way. We were to start at six next morning, and were to ride to snow-line and then betake ourselves to our feet. I went early to bed and dreamed of Itta and Dolly struggling up Mont Blanc, and that I was vainly trying to overtake them.

Shortly after 5 o'clock we were up and preparing for the expedition. I wore a short striped skirt of chintz, and my Norfolk jacket over a flannel shirt.

My boots, an old pair of patent leather ones, worn for
comfort in our long railway journeys, were extremely
unfit for rough walking. In a very broad-brimmed
hat and my thick veil, I fancy I looked the British
tourist, as depicted by *Punch*, to the life. Mr. B——
would insist on wearing a Scotch cap, in spite of our
remonstrances. As the glare of the sun on the snow
would be great, and good head-covering indis-
pensable, J—— took the precaution of carrying a
large silk bandana; he had climbed Swiss mountains
before, and knew what to expect. Oh, I must not
forget my umbrella, a faithful companion, from
which I never separated.

Our steeds and the guides waited at the Piazza; I
chose a nice little black mule in preference to the
peculiar three-cornered ponies. It was a lovely road,
or rather path, winding ever higher and higher
through pine woods, here and there interspersed
with an open common, covered with sweet-smelling
flowering bushes. There were bears and leopards to
be found, our guide told us, and in winter they
became quite daring, and would prowl round the
village at night in the hope of picking up a stray
child—or something.

The higher we got the rougher grew the pathway.
Big stones and rocks rolled from under the animals'
feet; they slipped and plunged along, always excepting my little black mule. She seemed to have the
feet of a cat. I gave her her own way entirely, and the
art with which she climbed over or up the hillside to
avoid obstacles was truly wonderful. A large tree had
fallen quite across the path at an awkward place. The
men got off and led the horses, but my mule
considered a moment, then bucked her fore-legs over,
and scrambling her hind-legs in some wonderful

manner she got over quite safely and went placidly on. By the time we reached snow-line most of the party, including our English acquaintances, had had enough of it. It certainly did look a formidable undertaking, and the guides were loud in their protests that we should not be able to get to the top, the snow was so deep. Some breakfast had been sent from the hotel, and this was then spread out. I declined to partake, feeling that I should require all my breath and agility if I was ever to reach the Observatory, but I wrapped up a biscuit and a piece of cheese and pocketed them, and secured a small flask of brandy.

Seeing we were determined, the guides then proceeded to fasten gunny-sacks to our feet. In reality they only tied them up in matting half-way to the knee, and they had not even brought matting enough, so sure were they that the snow-line would be the limit of the expedition. There were only five of us after all: J——, Mr. B——, myself, and two Americans, one from New York and the other, I think, a Brazilian. Our first climb was very severe, and nearly stopped our breath; but after a bit we got better, and went along at a good pace, till we reached the last crown of the Peak. The snow was very deep and not hard, and often I slipped through up to my waist, struggling out as best I could. The sun was scorching, and I felt grateful for my thick veil and the handkerchief round my neck. The umbrella had to be closed, as it was imposible to scramble along holding it up.

Mr. B—— kept well ahead, the rest of us together in straggling fashion. The guide was of no help to any one, and at last threw himself down and declared he was done. I must tell you that he had remained beind and eaten his luncheon, fully convinced that we should all come back; but finding we did not he had to hurry to overtake us. Fortunately we had the brandy; and a good dose of it had the desired effect, and enabled him to get along. Presently the Brazilian sat down and declared himself faint from hunger. He had eaten no second breakfast. Some brandy and my biscuit and piece of cheese restored him, and on we went. When not more than a quarter of a mile from the longed-for top I began to feel "done." My breath came in sobs—my feet felt like iron, and a terrible pain at my chest warned me to presevere all I knew. The telegraph wires now showed us the route, the poles sunken half-way in the snow. I resolved to go from one to another without stopping. Alas! I had to stop twice, and now the guide and the Brazilian collared me, passed me, and, to my bitter mortification, reached the door of the Observatory quite ten yards ahead! It was no use, I could get on no faster. I fancy we appeared forlorn objects to the two clerks who, poor souls, lived up at the top. It is the highest Observatory in the world, and the forecasts of the weather are taken from the top of Pike's Peak, one of the highest mountains in North America, 14,420 feet above the sea.

As to the view, I cannot describe it; it was wonderful! They said we could see for 150 miles over the Rockies—quite into Arizona, and I can believe that this was so. One peculiarity of it all was the striking clearness of everything. We could see Denver City, and even beyond, whilst Manitou, the Garden of the Gods, and all the weird scenery looked as plain as if we were there. The colouring was splendid. No words of mine can give the least idea of the glory of it all.

Our hosts hurried to make us some hot coffee, and to prepare us a meal; but we could not eat. The air affected us all more or less. I felt faint and painfully overcome with a desire to sleep, and we all had severe headaches. The only lively creature was a dear colley puppy. He did not seem to be at all affected by the air, and romped about in great delight at seeing new faces. The clerks told us they suffered terribly from headache, and were changed every three months, as their health could not stand the climate for a longer time. One of them died not long before. It must be a dreadful life.

Having rested for about half an hour, and written our names in the book, we prepared to descend. My gunny-bags were worn quite through, so I had no protection for my feet. Before starting they took us to an everlasting snow summit. When we looked down—standing on 100 ft. of frozen snow—into an endless crater, it made me shudder. One slip, and all would have been over! The remembrance of it comes back to me as a something never to be forgotten.

Of course, it was easier going down, but very tiring, and we tumbled into deep snowdrifts and struggled out as best we could. I was all the time nearly blind with a terrible headache. Glad, indeed, we were to reach the top of the last steep descent, and to see the timber line below us. I took hold of the telegraph wire—the posts stood about a yard and a-half above the snow—and, holding by it, fairly flew down, tumbling into a deep drift as I released my hold. The men sat down and slid to the bottom. I was helped on to my good little black mule, which with the horses had been left tied up to trees, and we began our descent. I really cannot remember how we got on. I let the mule take her own way, and sat

feeling bewildered and dazed till we got quite out of
the pine trees on to the flat. The air by this time was
no longer rarefied, and I gradually recovered. It was
as if a heavy weight had been lifted from my head.
Mr. B—— would not ride down. He tramped on and
actually got in before us.

Great was the excitement at the little hotel to
know how we had got on, and great was the surprise
expressed when, after a good hot bath and fresh
apparel, I took my place at the *table d'hôte* as fresh as
if I had done nothing out of the way. Poor Mr. B——
suffered terribly from sun-scorching. His face and
neck were severely blistered, and he was burnt a real
scarlet; glycerine and rose-water gave him a little
relief, but it was many days before he recovered from
the effects of the sun and snow combined. The poor
guide was snow-blind for some days, and the two
Americans went about wearing dark glasses, and
declared themselves quite knocked up. Thanks to the
precaution of wearing a thick veil and neckerchief, I
did not suffer in the least; indeed, I enjoyed the whole
thing thoroughly, and like to shut my eyes now to
recall the grand view and the marvellous colouring.

We returned to Cheyenne shortly after the expedition, and found the weather as bad as when we left.
This was the third week in May, and we had quite a
heavy snow storm; one night it was so cold I was glad
of the stove in my room. J—— was suffering from a
rather bad ulcerated throat, which we could not help
connecting in some way with the unsanitary
arrangements of our hotel, and we were very anxious
to make a start; but we were kept nearly a week
before any change of weather showed itself. At last
the sun shone again, and in a few hours we were
quite in midsmmer heat. It was a lovely day when,

having packed our very scanty allowance of luggage at the back of our buckboard, and the bedding, rugs, etc., on to the buggy—which, with its team of four bays, looked really quite imposing—we started again, in fine style, and drove through Cheyenne at a rapid pace away on to the vast rolling prairies. J—— and I were in the buckboard, drawn by a most excellent pair of dun 14-hand cobs— "buckskins," as they call them out West—named respectively Charlie and Frank. Charlie and I became great friends during our travels, but Frank was not of a responsive nature, and showed an equal disregard for caresses and sugar. Game, grand little steeds, I never knew them flag through the longest journeys, and over roads (or, rather, bad land) that here in England we should deem it madness to attempt to drive over. They certainly were the best little horses in the world.

We had 50 good miles to do before we reached our first halting place for the night—Mr. Kelly's Ranche; but we had luncheon at Horse Creek. Our hostess was an Indian woman, married to an American; their daughter, a comely girl about 15 years of age, was also married to an American. We had a very good lunch—roast beef, potatoes, stewed plums, and good bread and butter. A few miles before we reached Horse Creek we met Mr. Frewen and Mr. Hay, returning from their ranche.

They gave us a dismal account of bad roads, rivers flooded, and various difficulties, not to say dangers, we should encounter, and strongly advised my returning to Cheyenne. This of course I would not do; so after a pleasant chat we parted company, meeting a little further on another trap, with a coffin slung under it. It seems that during a snow storm two men were on the hunt after some horses, and lost their way. They had only one horse between them, so the older man persuaded the younger one, a new hand at the work, to let him ride on and seek the run-aways, whilst the other was to remain stationary and fire his gun at intervals. This he did, but as time passed and his comrade did not return, and the cold was becoming intense, he determined to try and find his way back to camp. Unfortunately he had lent his chaps, or leather outer trousers, to his friend, and his knife was in the pockets. His feet, in their heavy leather boots, began to freeze, and he could not get their fastenings undone. Helplessly crippled he could go no further, and two days after was discovered all but dead, his feet and legs frozen to his knees. They got him to the little inn at Fort Laramie, and here he had both legs amputated; but all in vain, the poor fellow never rallied, and it was his corpse we passed. His comrade was found about 300 yards from the spot with three horses lying round him all dead. It was supposed they had been killed by lightning, as a fearful storm was raging at the time.

It was an uninteresting drive to Kelly's, over a jolting, flat country. I drove nearly all the way. We found quite a nice house, and J—— and I had a small sitting room given up to us to sleep in. A mattress, pillows, and blankets were placed on the floor, my last experience of a luxurious bed for many nights to come. After a pleasant supper in the public room the men retired to smoke, and I climbed to the top of some distant bluffs to see the sun set, which he did in clouds of crimson and gold. I thought of all the dear ones at home, and what they were probably doing, till dreading to become sentimental I retraced my steps, and shortly after was sleeping the sleep of the just, till I was aroused by the tramp of feet and the sound of wheels outside. Getting up I peeped through the blinds and saw four men bringing out another coffin, which was placed in a waggon, and, after some directions, driven off the way we had come. I must confess to having felt a little uncomfortable. A coffin seemed such an ordinary way of getting folks home out here; but I consoled myself by thinking that we could not possibly have any more "blizzards" in June, so were not likely to get frost-bitten.

By seven next morning we were all up and ready to start. Such a cold, raw morning, I was glad of my fur cloak. It threatened a storm of some kind, and, just as we reached a little road ranche for luncheon about twelve, down came the rain in a perfect deluge. We were glad to be under shelter; but of luncheon I could not partake, except a cup of coffee. It was such a dirty place, and I had not got used to the rough Western ways, nor had my appetite become, as it afterwards did, like a ravenous wolf's, eager to devour anything. The weather cleared in a little while, and after a narrow escape from sticking in a hole, fording the creek (a team of mules in front of us stuck fast), we drove on; but the mud was fearful—it flew up all over us. Fort Laramie was our destination, and was a good 40-mile drive. The road became very rough, and going down a steep pitch we nearly had a nasty accident. A telegraph wire had partly given way, and hung across our path just at the level of the horses' heads. We were going a good pace—I was driving—when suddenly, to my surprise, J—— seized the reins and brought us to a stand. As it was, Charlie was nearly choked, and Frank's temper upset at being so roughly stopped. I resigned the reins to J—— after this, and it was fortunate that I did. We were driving over a broken-down sort of trail, with banks on either side. Suddenly the path ceased, and a chasm of fully a yard yawned in front,—a deep rift. What were we to do? Turn we could not; we had only one choice, to jump it. My heart stood still. Putting their sagacious heads down to see what it was, our good buckskins pulled themselves together and leapt clean over, pulling us behind with a fearful jerk; but in landing on the hard, flint-like sand Charlie's feet slipped, and he fell on his side. But he was up in an instant, and, just as our hind wheels were slipping back into the rift, with a tremendous spring the pair carried us once more on to *terra firma*, and away we went, as gaily as before. I do not pretend for an instant that I liked the incident, but it was one of those dangers there was no way out of except going through it. I expected a smash-up, and was truly relieved when all was so well over.

We halted at a neat little road ranche at Fort Laramie, where we got good stabling and corn for our horses, and a good supper and bed rooms for ourselves. We strolled out to the barracks afterwards to hear the band play, and then on to a hill to see the coffin wherein Spotted Tail's daughter is buried. The Indians do not bury their dead; they have an open coffin, in which the corpse is laid and with her, her blankets, ornaments, and little articles she valued. The coffin is placed on four poles about 7 ft. high, and the corpse is left for the birds to pick at. The winds of heaven scatter the poor garments abroad; but it is sacred so far that no hand touches anything. It all moulders away. We climbed up and looked in, but only the bones and some beads remained of the poor Indian maiden whose really sad story I must now relate.

Some years ago a young American officer, shooting in Indian territory, fell in with a party of Indians. As they were friendly and inclined to assist him in his search for game he remained with them for some time. Spotted Tail was the chief—a great brave—and Spotted Tail's daughter was the fairest maiden of the tribe. Needless to say the young officer made a deep impression upon her young heart. Possibly she mistook the natural courtesy and kindness with which he treated her for a warmer feeling. Indian women are not accustomed to gentle treatment at the hands of their lords and masters. When, at the end of his expedition, the young officer returned to his camp at Fort Laramie he left a desolate heart behind. Twice did the poor girl endeavour to follow him, and twice was she stopped and brought back. At last she managed to escape, and set off on foot in search of her love. How she contrived to trace him no one can tell; but some two months after she left her tribe she reached Laramie, in a state of utter exhaustion, during a heavy fall of snow. Poor thing! in spite of her efforts she never looked on the loved face; her strength failed, and she fell exhausted on the summit of the small hill overlooking the Fort. She was not discovered for a few days, when life was, of course, extinct. Her father and some of his tribe, who had followed her, with the hope, no doubt, of effecting some arrangement with the officer, only came in time to perform the funeral ceremonies. She was buried, or rather laid out, in her open coffin, on the spot where she died, a sad example of misplaced love and devotion.

When we returned to our inn we found an officer waiting for our party, with an invitation to the mess, or club. I, of course, remained, and had a pleasant chat with our little hostess till the men came back. I did not quite like the look of the bed the good woman had provided for our night's repose, with its dingy sheets; and as it was quite chilly, I wrapped myself in my fur cloak, and lay down outside the bed clothes. I had not slept an hour before a disagreeable sensation aroused me, and I knew my tormentors were about. Springing up, I lighted my candle. Ugh! the whole place swarmed with horrid little bugs; they were running about, and getting back into the chinks of the wooden walls as fast as they could, alarmed at the light. Of course, sleep was out of the question for me. Envying J——, who reposed calmly and quite unmolested, I dressed, and looked at the watch a quarter to one. I went into the sitting room and tried the little horsehair sofa; but this was no better than my bed, as the horrid creatures lived in the wooden walls, and came out as soon as I was quiet. Eventually I carried out the least uncomfortable seat I could find, and, wrapped in my cloak, spent the remainder of the night *al fresco*. And a long and weary time it seemed till day broke, when I ventured in again and had an hour's blessed sleep on the sofa, only disturbed at last by the good woman of the house, who came to light her stove, and was greatly surprised at finding me dressed and asleep on the sofa, and none the less so when I explained why, as somehow the people who live in these wooden houses either get used to the infliction or escape it altogether. Anyway, whenever we halted for the night at a road ranche I always made my bed up outside, preferring mosquitos or even snakes, to the odious inhabitant of the red wood huts.

After a substantial and well-cooked breakfast we
started again. This time I went with the four-in-
hand, and J—— and Mr. B—— followed in the buckboard. We had a long drive before us, and the country
was very pretty. Trees and rivers—the latter easily
forded—such rich pasture, and herds of cattle
grazing; and we also saw several antelopes grazing
amongst them. I think we went over some of Mr.
Ulrich's ground. The cattle were wild, and fled as we
came near. It was very hot and sultry, and I was glad
of a halt. About one o'clock we chose a pretty spot
amongst the cotton trees, close to a delicious stream,
which unfortunately looked better than it tasted.
Our horses appreciated it, however, and that was the
great thing. It was difficult to get them all tethered
apart, and one, called "Old Soldier," broke loose, and
galloped off kicking. Luckily his comrades called
loudly after him, and whether his conscience
reproached him with deserting his friends, or their
entreaties prevailed, I cannot say, but back he came,
and allowed himself to be fastened to the team.

I here made the first trial of my Etna for making
tea, and I am bound to say a more annoying machine
was never invented. The amount of spirit it took to
boil the water, the way in which the light went out at
a moment's notice, and, above all, the time it took to
heat the water, was always a joke against me
whenever we halted for a meal; but I would not be
defeated, and found at last that the only good plan
was to dig a hole in the sand, and place the Etna in it.
This kept the wind away, and if the sand did not fall
in too much, I generally managed to give them a
fairly good cup of tea in about twenty minutes. We
thoroughly enjoyed our pic-nic and the rest, sitting
round and talking over our plans, till suddenly and

without warning a vivid flash, followed by a peal of thunder, startled us to our feet, and to the consciousness that a fearful black storm was hurrying towards us. I packed up with celerity, whilst the men hastened to hitch up, first watering all the horses again. It is a fact that during these long drives the horses are allowed to drink as much as they wish at every opportunity; and in our case no ill effect was observable, thus flatly contradicting the idea that horses are not to drink during a long journey, or at most only a mouthful to freshen them. We put on our slickers, got out our waterproof aprons, made ourselves snug, and started.

Oh, what a storm it was! The lightning played about the harness, and seemed at times to fall in forked vividness close to us; the thunder crashed and roared, and down came a deluge of rain. It was so dark we could only just distinguish the herds of cattle tearing past, and a troop of frightened deer that came nearly over us. It was truly grand; but it did not last long, for in less than an hour all was calm and serene, the sun shining again brightly, though we heard the thunder growling in the distance for some time.

We had got out of the varied bluff country, and now drove for a long way across flat uninteresting plains till we reached the enclosure of Player's Ranche, our destination for the night. 50,000 acres are enclosed with a ring fence, and as this was a new purchase of our manager's, we were anxious to inspect a part of it. We drove some six or seven miles along a good track before reaching the ranche, a fair-sized wooden house, standing in a separate enclosure, with good stabling and barns a short way off. Out came Mr. Pfost, the foreman, a good-looking Swede, who greeted us quite cordially; two other men took charge of the horses, and we went inside. Anything more uncomfortable at first sight I never saw. A large room, with a very dirty floor, a wooden table and some benches, a sink at one end for washing purposes, and wooden frames for eight beds one above the other at one side of the room. It was my first actual experience of roughing it; a little later on and I recognised Player's Ranche as a luxurious abode compared to some we stopped at. At the back was a small room opening into the kitchen; this was the dining room, and but for the heat and the dirty floor it was a good enough room. So it was settled that I could sleep there on my air bed, and the men would manage all together in the big general room.

I proceeded to get out what was wanted from our luggage. I always changed my dress for dinner when possible, and was glad to get off my thick homespun riding and walking suit, which was too hot really for the climate, and into a plain linen tea dress I had bought at Cheyenne. Mr. R—— and I were both suffering from our eyes, the combined effects of alkali dust and glare of sun, and J——'s throat was still bad, so I had to attend to the ailments as well as to the wardrobes. After that I made some really good tea in the kitchen, and as we had milk as well as sugar with it, it was a treat. The cook, an Irishman—and such a quaint little felow!—provided an excellent supper of cornflour porridge, new hot rolls, bacon and eggs, and grape jelly. But we were not hungry, and rather out of sorts, so after supper I strolled out to the river, and watched the sun set, whilst the men looked after the horses and settled the plans for the next day. J—— and Mr. B—— had a game of chess by the light of a solitary dip. Mr. Pfost, Mr. R—— and I discussed American life *versus*

English ditto till about ten, when in came the outside men, bringing rugs for the beds. Mr. B—— blew out my air bed for me, and we arranged it on the table; then, when all the lights were out—as, though there was a window, there was no blind—I brought a big kettle of hot water out of the kitchen and enjoyed the luxury of a delicious bath in the gutta percha bath we carried. I had to prop the outer door open, it was so insufferably hot, but as nothing worse than a big toad was likely to come in it did not matter. Though I was very tired, the excitement and newness of everything kept me awake, and notwithstanding I had spent the night before on my chair out of doors I could not rest, and was really glad to be up and dressed a little before six, so as to be out of the way of the cook, who was to come at six to light the stove and prepare breakfast. When he came he insisted on carrying out my bath himself, and, in consequence, one of the wooden supports slipped, and down it went, deluging the place with water. He remarked, whilst mopping it up, "Well, it's not often it gets a bit of a wash, so it won't do *much* harm."

The weather had changed, and in the night a storm had raged again, and everything was very wet outside. J—— and Mr. B—— went to bathe at the stream, and for breakfast we had a repetition of the supper, only coffee was served instead of tea. We went out to watch the men drive in the horses for our ride round the demesne. My steed was a quiet little mare, with her foal at her foot, and a yearling and a two-year-old also trotting with her, so we were quite a family party. The rest were mounted on fairly good ponies; Mr. Pfost on a big black mule. We rode first to the water flume, which would be a very real advantage to the place when finished, and then to the water boundary. Such rich pasture land it all was, and near the stream was the hay land. Mr. R—— calculated that they would make some hundreds of tons that season. It simply requires cutting, the sun dries it thoroughly in two days, and then it is stacked as it stands. It was blazing hot, and after some three and a-half hours' ride we were glad to get under shelter again. After luncheon, we once more packed up our things, and then bidding adieu to the foreman—a much better kind of man then it was usual to meet with—we started for our own ranche, the Neobrara, or Running Water. I drove Charlie and Frank, Mr. B—— with me, and as the water in the creek was very high, the banks very steep, and the horses plunged down suddenly, I nearly over-balanced and tumbled in. We were well splashed; but it made us laugh heartily at the ridiculous figures we made, clinging to the rail with despairing energy. It was only a thirty-mile drive that day, and the ponies, who knew every yard of the road, trotted along, pulling double. We forded the creek, and just as the rain began we reached our destination, to my mind the most charming spot in the world. We had travelled 175 miles from Cheyenne, and were to rest a few days before going on to the Platt River Round-up.

I must try and give some idea of the Neobrara Ranche and the country round it. Not a bit flat, much resembling Scotch lowland scenery, a broad green valley, through which a bright little trout stream wound its way, and along its banks we put up ducks, herons, and other water fowl. The hills rose in high undulations for ever and ever,—a country where one would get lost easily in an hour when once out of sight of the ranche and its enclosures. The buildings

were divided, one neat little wooden two-roomed
house, with windows glazed and made to open, at one
end of the square enclosure; at the other, excellent
stabling for twelve horses, and a stock yard; in the
centre the kitchen, which contained an excellent
range and quite a respectable show of pots and
kettles; then the dining room, and through this the
sleeping room for the men. My room, besides two
windows, contained a nice little stove (it was quite
chilly enough at night to appreciate a small wood
fire), a wooden bedstead in one corner (which Mr.
R——made most comfortable with a buffalo rug and
J——'s blankets), a rocking chair, a table, and two or
three seats. I always slept on the floor on my air bed
and the lovely soft Cheyenne blankets; I had become
quite reconciled to the absence of sheets. In the day
time the air bed did duty as a sofa, covered up with a
bright rug or two, as this room was our drawing room
as well; and very neat it always looked, decorated
with the flowers which I gathered on the hills, where
they bloomed in profusion. They were of the common
kind, but very bright and pretty. Our cook was a
splendid felow, and prided himself on giving us as
great a variety as was possible. His hot cakes—something between a sponge and a pound cake—were
most excellent, and his bread was the lightest I ate
anywhere in America; and this is saying a great deal,
as they certainly do excel in the art of bread making.

After packing and changing our things we were
quite glad of "supper," as it is called, though the meal
was served at six o'clock. We had fried beef and
potatoes, poached eggs and bacon, excellent butter
and milk and coffee, tinned grapes and hot cake. The
only two men left on the ranche, Charlie—a German,
who was carter and horse manager—and a queer

little Irishman, sat below the salt, as it were. Bury, our cook, waited on us, but sitting down, and all joined in the conversation if it suited them, or they had time. After "supper" it rained again, so we took refuge in the sitting room, and played some merry rubbers. Later on I made tea on the stove, and at about ten o'clock we all retired for the night. I should have slept very well, being tired, but for the little wee ants that invaded me—tiny little atoms, which did not bite but kept me in a continual state of irritation. However, next day I gave the room a thorough cleaning out, and was scarcely disturbed again. I enjoyed our few days here very much; we rode nearly every day. Mr. B—— and J—— scrambled amongst the hills, and tried to shoot wild ducks or an antelope, but only succeeded in bringing down a redwinged starling. These are such pretty birds; some have yellow wings instead of red. I cured my wings, and have them still. I hunted for wild flowers, helped Bury to milk the cows, and washed all the clothes ready for our start, and, in short, led the simplest and wildest of lives, in the purest and most delicious air I ever breathed. The men of our party played chess, had long discussions on the best way of doing what was before us, wrote long letters, and at night we had whist of the most unscientific kind. The one drawback was the non-arrival of the mail. Twice did Charlie drive the waggon over to Fort Robinson, some twenty-five miles off, and twice did he return empty handed, to our real disappointment.

At length we could wait no longer, so at nine o'clock on a bright morning we started for the big Round-up, in the buggy and backboard. We took a little tent, which added greatly to the load and to our discomfort, and as we only once used it we resolved to

risk the hot nights and leave it behind on our return.
J—— drove me with two grey horses, Charlie and
Steel. Charlie behaved like a mad horse at first,
plunging and tearing down the hills, his head in the
air and quite unmanageable. He was a Broncho, and
never could get used to the ways of men; in addition
to this he had been on the Round-up, and his poor
mouth was dreadfully sore from the sudden checks
the men give their horses; but at our first halt we
changed his bit for a gutta percha one, which Mr.
R—— always used with his buckskins, and he went
much better—indeed, his mouth got quite healed by
the end of the journey. It was very rough going, and
we jolted terribly. I was thankful for my air cushion
and pillow, but I got some severe bruises against the
iron rail at the side, and sometimes had to hold on for
dear life. We lunched by the stream, under a broiling
sun; it was too hot to eat, but the grass was good, and
we here made the discovery that Charlie would eat
no corn—would not look at it. This was bad, as of
course at night he ought to be resting instead of
eating; however, there was no help for it.

Having rested two hours, we packed up again and
started off. The country was uninteresting. We met
some unhappy emigrants making their slow way to
some distant parts. Poor souls! their El Dorado
would, I fear, turn out a sad disappointment. We had
a little chat with them to cheer them up. The heat
was awful, and we gladly hailed a distant growl of
thunder. At the same time we prepared to receive
rain, and none too soon. Down it came in a real
torrent, drenching everything—corn bags, tents, and
traps. And such lightning and thunder! On we drove,
and very thankful we were to reach Red Willows, our
destination for the night, at about seven o'clock. By

this time it was quite cold, so the big stove was
lighted at once. Whilst the men attended to the
horses I got out the wet garments and hung them
round the fire, making a steam you could hardly see
through. Our costumes at supper were, to say the
least, quaint, as wet boots and stockings had to be
discarded, and slippers and knickerbocker breeches
had a very funny appearance. I was decidedly the
best off on this occasion.

Two other travellers who had come by stage from
Sydney had taken refuge at the Red Willows, and,
first come being first served, they had secured the one
bed room. Major Paddock, however, was a true
soldier, and offered to give it up to me at once. Of
course, I declined—I think a little to his relief—and
we became great friends, and before we parted we
had promised to break our journey at Fort Robinson
after our return from the Round-up on the Platt, and
when we were really making our way to Spearfish.
We all slept in the sitting room, J—— and I on a sofa
that opened into a kind of double bed—but too
uncomfortable even to endure—Messrs. R—— and
B—— on the floor on the air bed. After courting sleep
for some time in vain, I got up, lighted the little lamp,
and sat in the rocking chair reading till day dawned,
when the stage came rumbling in, and the Major and
his son departed. I was so dead beat I lay outside his
bed, and fell sound asleep till the sun came shining
full upon me. Seeing a lovely high hill in front of the
house I hurried through my dressing, and proceeded
to climb to the top. Such a splendid morning after the
storm, and such a grand view all round. I came upon
several rabbits, just like those at home, and a lot of
flowers and ferns, and descended to breakfast at
about seven o'clock, hungry as a hunter.

We were packed up and off again by about eight
o'clock, and drove through a charming rugged
country, along a fairly good road, till about twelve,
when we came upon the Platt River. It is a wide, very
shallow, slow running stream, very muddy, and with
steep banks. A difficult river to water the horses in,
as we found, and quite different to our English ideas
of a river. The country was flat and not pretty at all,
and the heat great, in spite of a strong wind that
prevented my making tea in the Etna. At last I
scooped a deep hole in the sand, and so managed to
produce a little after nearly half-an-hour's worry. I
often regretted not having brought a good machine
from England. The tea was our one luxury, but the
trouble of making it and the time it took were
wearisome, and sometimes complete failure was the
result of my exertions.

After driving a couple of hours, we at last came
upon the "Round-up," and a curious sight it was.
Almost as far as eye could see were vast herds of
cattle streaming slowly along. Mr. R—— calculated
there were some twenty thousand. The incessant
bellowing sounded formidable, and the appearance
of the cattle was not reassuring, for though not large
their huge wide-spread horns and wild eyes made me
rather glad to be in the buggy. Really they were
much too frightened to be savage, though at times a
cow with her calf by her side, or when separated from
it, would charge anything. A dog would be destroyed
at once, and though on horseback you may ride quite
close up to a herd, a man on foot would cause such a
panic that a general stampede would no doubt be the
result. We drew up to watch them cutting out some
cattle from the large herd. It certainly was very
cleverly done. Two men rode right in amongst them

till they got close to the particular beast they wanted; they then quietly forced him along till quite outside the rest, when they yelled and shouted like demons. The poor steer, terrified, tore off at a gallop, pursued by the men. His object was to get back to his comrades and theirs to prevent him. Once they had got him up to the small bunch of cattle that he belonged to, and all was well, but frequently he dodged them, and in spite of their frantic galloping, their awful oaths and yells, he got back to the large herd, and all had to be done over again.

I could not help thinking that were the whole thing done more quietly and gently much time might be saved, as the cowboys so terrify the wretched beasts that they become like mad things. However, the cowboy is a strange creature, quite unlike any other of his fellow men, and all he does must be done with swagger and noise. Their riding did not impress me. To begin with, the ponies are poor little things, about 14 hands, generally speaking utterly broken-spirited; and their saddles struck me as next to impossible to fall out of. Such a high croup behind, and a huge pommel in front, where the lasso is twisted—quite different to our saddles, where men must ride by balance. However, though I never saw any clever horsemanship, I was told wonderful stories of bucking horses which if *non è vero è ben trovato*, and the cowboys should be Centaurs to be able to ride them.

I did not like the cowboys; they impressed me as brutal and cowardly, besides being utterly devoid of manners or good feeling. This was pretty well exemplified on our reaching our own outfit, where we were to spend the night. We drove up to unhitch, but though Mr. R—— was well known to all the boys and the foreman, not a soul came forward to offer to help us; they stood looking on whilst we took out the teams, unharnessed and tethered them, driving in pegs for the purpose. They watched me with a bucket and rope make some ineffectual efforts to draw water. Nay, when we began to put up our tent (by the way, we did use it one night), a work of much labour, as the ground was so hard and the pegs took so much driving in (I know I hurt my hands considerably in doing this), not a man offered to help me. I mention this because we hear so much of the chivalrous cowboy and his great admiration and attention to everything in the shape of a woman, or "lady," I ought to say. Well, I can only say that in England, Scotland or Ireland, the humblest labourer, gillie or lounger that walks would have come forward to offer, at any rate, to help a woman as a simple matter of course; but in free America, where everyone aims at independence, a man dreads an act of courtesy of this kind, lest his fellow men might imagine he was derogating from his standard of equality. Our good old saying, that "Gold cannot tarnish," would have no meaning for them.

I *was* tired; we had jolted over a hundred miles in our two days' drive, and the heat and sleepless night and indifferent food were very trying. Still, I was quite prepared to enjoy the evening, only it was not enjoyable. Shortly after we had got all fixed for the night we were called to supper at the waggon. A fire was lighted in a hole, and some strips of awfully tough beef were cooked over it.

The cook was a poor bread maker, and the loaf more resembled dough than bread. A curious mixture of apples, currants, and treacle formed our feast. I dared not produce my knife and fork case, for fear of giving offence, and as the knives were cleaned by the simple process of sticking them in the ground I confess I did not greatly care to use them. The coffee was hot and strong, and this made up for a good deal. I do not pretend to say it was clear, neither had we any milk. However, supper was got through, and then we sat on logs by the fire, and tried to get the men to talk; but not a word would they say, except "Yes" and "No." Mr. R—— said had I not been there they would have talked, but they feared their language might shock me! It was certainly a lovely and picturesque sight—the river glistening in the bright full moonlight, the white tents and waggons, the camp fires burning at intervals for over a mile, the background of hills looking snow-white under the moonshine, and the huge herds of cattle, with the mounted guard of cowboys in their picturesque dress, to say nothing of the herds of horses enclosed and feeding round, made up a scene I shall never forget, and which quite atoned for the discomforts and fatigues we had undergone.

Early to bed was the order of the night, as very early to rise is likewise the practice; so by nine we sought our tent. Mr. R—— slept with his foreman, and Mr. B——, J——, and I shared the tent. The mosquitos were very bad, I suppose from our being so close to the water, and they at last fairly drove me out of my bed and the tent. Once outside, the fresh wind dispersed them. The mist was rising so thickly about a yard from the ground that it hid everything, and a peculiarly nasty smell pervaded the air. I fancy it must have been rather unhealthy. I did not go far from the tent for fear of disturbing the cattle, whose incessant lowing made me melancholy, but I sat me down by the fast-dying embers, and my thoughts flew

over the sea, wishing it were possible for some of my
friends at home to possess the wonderful mirror that
reflected what those who were absent were doing. It
would have surprised, and I think rather delighted
them, could they have looked upon that midnight
scene.

I am so often asked what *is* a Round-up that I will
try and describe it for the benefit of those who may
care to read about it. To begin with, the land where
the cattle feed belongs to no one in particular; the
herds are bought, not the land (I am not speaking of
Texas and Indian territory, as I believe there the
land is bought as well), consequently no one fences
the cattle in. They roam all the winter where they
will, and sometimes, in a severe season, will drift
before the storms for long distances, as much as 150
miles from their ranche. It is necessary to collect
them every summer to brand the calves, and also to
drive them nearer home; but as this would be too
great an undertaking for one proprietor, four or five
will join outfits for the search. An outfit for a big
round-up like that we were on should consist of a
large waggon and four horses, or mules. This waggon
carries the fire-wood, provisions, cooking utensils,
and bedding—and a tight fit it is to get all in. Very
heavy and arduous is the task of dragging it through
and over every sort of bad land, and crossing swollen
rivers. The cook is driver, and generally manages
alone. Besides this, there will be a foreman and from
eight to twelve other men, each of whom must have
at least six ponies; they ride by night and by day, and
change the ponies at least four times each day. It is
frightfully hard work for the ponies, this severe and
constant galloping, to say nothing of the strain upon
their legs when the rider is lassoing the cattle; and

the greyhound-like action these ponies have to display in turning with the cattle, and racing to part them off from the herd, is truly marvellous. The riders are, as a rule, big men, and the saddle weighs many pounds, so my readers will readily understand how a couple of hours of this kind of thing is quite as much as the grass-fed, undersized little animals can manage at a time.

As soon as all are assembled at a given point on a certain day the hunt begins. The riders scour the country far and near in a wide semicircle, driving all the cattle they find before them, and always making for a given point. Those outfits whose ranches are not so distant generally cut out their own cattle and drive them in in separate bunches; and this is the great difficulty, as the beasts are always trying to rejoin the big herd, and it is constant work, day and night, to prevent this. When a sufficient number are collected a halt is called, and all the poor calves are branded with the owner's name or mark; then they are safe, as, even did some adventurous spirit collect a bunch of cattle and ship them as his own to Chicago, he would gain nothing, as the purchaser would pay the money into the bank for the proper owner, whose brand is registered and perfectly known. This registration is undertaken by a company called, I believe, "The Wyoming Cattle Association," and of course every rancheman belongs to it. This will explain what puzzles many people so much, namely, what it is that prevents the cattle being stolen on such a wild range. Of course, now and again cattle are stolen for food, both by Indians and white men, but this loss is calculated upon much in the same way as a hen wife calculates to lose some chickens by hawks, cats, or foxes. If unbranded cattle are found straying they may be claimed by the owner of the herd they are with, and are termed "may-ounks;" they form a fair percentage of gain, as of course it is impossible to find *all* the cattle; they increase and multiply, and sometimes a cow with four unbranded calves has been discovered by a lucky ranche owner.

When the Round-up is ended—*i.e.*, the whole body having reached their final destination—a general division takes place, the cows and calves are let loose, and the steers also, except those meant for market. These are driven off by the owner's men, and the remainder of the men return to their respective ranches, or are dismissed for the season. The cattle travel slowly—ten miles in a long day—feeding as they go, till the depôt is reached, where they are embarked in trucks and taken to Chicago, and there their poor lives are ended. It is a cruel business at best, and the misery the poor things undergo in the cars is terrible. Some owners are erecting huge sheds for keeping and feeding the cattle in through the winter, and the poor brutes thus get used to the loss of freedom and sight of men, and the journey is not the terror and misery it must be to these wild creatures. Other owners, also, are taking to slaughter at their ranches, or at the depôt, and then send the dead meat to its destination, thus avoiding the heavy loss in condition *en route* to Chicago. This treatment is far more merciful.

A cowboy gets from fifty to sixty dollars a month whilst on the Round-up; and this sum is well earned, for it is a hard, rough life, and very trying. They are constantly getting wet through, and this, in the end, tells on the strongest of constitutions. Advantages they certainly have—namely, as much food as they can eat, and no drink stronger than coffee. Unfortunately, they make up for this enforced abstinence by indulging in tremendous drinking bouts whenever they take a holiday. They make for Cheyenne, Miles City, or some other bar-infested town. Indeed, if a round-up is stopped by stress of weather within distance of any town, or "city," as it is styled, there is no keeping the cowboy from his "spree," and many a desperate deed has been done by these mad drunkards, and many a life taken in "fun." In old days these disgraceful scenes were of frequent occurrence.

To resume my narrative, I had regained the tent and fallen asleep at last, in spite of the mosquitoes, and was most unwillingly aroused by Mr. R—— calling out, "Breakfast! breakfast! Get up and hear the birds sing." Not that there were any birds to sing, but it sounded inviting. I looked at my watch. Just three o'clock; but it was broad daylight, and the sun was rising in gold and crimson—a glorious sight enough. All were up and about outside, and it was amusing to watch the horses drawn into an imaginary circle and lassoed. Two men hold a long rope, one end tied to the waggon in a half triangle, and the horses seemed to think they were enclosed all round, and made no effort to get away. Finding a quantity of dough on the waggon flap I speedily made friends with some of the ponies, and presently they came crowding round quite friendly and anxious for a piece. I have since heard that the cook was furious at my giving his bread away in this fashion, and the foreman told Mr. R—— that some of the horses I was coaxing and feeding would not let a boy handle them in that manner for anything. I believe firmly the

animal creation instinctively recognises those who
are fond of them.

Breakfast was a repetition of the dinner; but I had
suffered so fearfully from indigestion that I ab-
stained from touching the dough, and actually
breakfasted off a small piece of tough beef and some
coffee. Fancy this at three o'clock in the morning; but
the keen air made us all ravenous. There was to be no
more rounding-up for a few days. The men were busy
clearing off the different bunches of cattle, and some
of the outfits, being near their own ranges, left, after
getting their herds pretty well together. We also
packed up our tent and belongings, and started back
for the Red Willows. It was very very hot, and the
flies were tormenting. There is a horrid pest called
buffalo-fly, a tiny thing smaller than a midge, but the
venom it imparts to its bites is wonderful, and these
insects creep everywhere—into the hair, down the
collars and cuffs—and drive one nearly crazy. The
buffalo dreads it, and a herd will stampede for miles
to escape its irritation.

We got along very slowly, as poor Charlie was
beginning to flag terribly. He would not eat the grass
when we halted for luncheon, and shortly after we
again started it was evident he could go no further.
This was very awkward, as we were in the midst of
the prairies and quite thirty miles from Red Willows.
Mr. R—— decided to make for the nearest coach
station (which was in the opposite direction), and try
to get a fresh horse. J—— and I were to drive on with
the sound pair to Red Willows, which we succeeded in
doing, only losing our road once. We struck the track
made by the Sydney coach, and got on capitally, even
overtaking the huge mail coach, with its four horses,
and getting in first to Red Willows, so that we were

able to bespeak the bedroom this time. As it was only six in the afternoon, (by the way, we had been travelling from five in the morning), after seeing the horses well fed and attended to, I set off to climb the hills, so as to command a good view of the road our fellow travellers would be likely to take on their return. We had induced the hostess, as a huge favour, to put off supper till seven. It was a lovely evening, and quite delicious up on the heights, steep, rocky, volcanic elevations one above the other, and much more difficult to reach than I expected. Having got at last to the top, I remained some time watching and waiting, till the sun began to sink and the wind to blow chilly, but no trace of our companions could be seen.

On my return I found supper all laid and waiting, although only J—— and I were to partake of it; but we were anxious about the absentees, and our appetites had left us. It turned very cold and threatened a storm, and was altogether getting a dreary evening. We found some books and old papers, which we sat reading till about half-past ten, going continually to the door to listen, for it had become pitch dark. At about eleven o'clock we were preparing to turn in, when, oh, joy! the sound of wheels coming nearer reached us, and out we rushed. There were our companions at last; poor souls, dead beat, and rather cross. Of course, the horses were their first care. I saw at a glance Grey Charlie was not there, but did not ask any questions, busying myself with getting the coffee warmed up on the stove, and such supper as I could find, the landlord and landlady being in bed asleep; but when the poor souls came in they could not eat a mouthful, but drank deeply of milk and water. I had made the sofa bed as comfortable as possible, and in less time than it has taken me to write this they were rolled in their blankets and enjoying their well-earned rest. Twenty hours of pretty hard work on a minimum of food is enough to try the strongest constitution.

We were none of us awake very early next day, but over some excellent hot coffee and new rolls we heard the story of their adventures. It seems Charlie was "Lokood"—*i.e.*, poisoned by a herb of that name. It acts as a soporific, and sometimes is deadly in its results. They got him to the river and he drank, and then had a great roll, which seemed to do him good, and they then managed, slowly and laboriously, to get him along, his comrade Antelope doing all the work as far as the coach station, when poor Charlie gave in, and was left on the prairie. I may say that subsequently he got all right, and was brought by the outfit back to Neobrara.

The only procurable horse was a young unbroken four-year-old mare! She, however, was very reasonable, and allowed herself to be harnessed quietly, and, after a frightful plunging and tearing at first, finally settled down and brought them along famously; but poor Antelope was quite done long before they got in, and hence the delay. It really was a rash undertaking; but there was no help for it, and it proves the old proverb, "Dieu aide qui s'aide." Fancy in England starting after dark to climb over a very hilly and difficult road with an unbroken four-year-old!

The mare was returned next day, and we were able to hire a good brown horse to continue our journey; but it was after ten when we started, and we had fifty very rough miles between us and Neobrara, the first twenty-five of which were really dreadful work for

87

the horses, and the jolting was something inde-scribable. We stopped for lunch close by the Dead-wood Coach Station, as there was a well but no windlass, so we had to tie Antelope to the end of a rope and make him draw the buckets. The heat was killing and the insects something to remember. Our next halt was at Running Water Ranche, kept by a cheery little Welsh woman and her husband, a poor paralytic. His brother seemed the true master of the house, and he and she made a good business with their cattle and providing for the passengers on the stage coach which ran from Sydney to Deadwood.

The woman was delighted to talk with us about Wales and the old country, brought us out some excellent home-made blackberry cordial, and pres-ently gave us a capital supper. We had only some twelve miles more, but it was getting late and I was sadly tired.

When we started again it was nearly dark, and we had to keep calling to Mr. R——, who drove in front, as there was no road, and we should have soon lost our way amongst the sand hills. The summer light-ning was flashing in the horizon, and now and then a flame of forked electricity seemed to fall at one's very feet. It was lovely and wonderful, but foretold a storm, and right glad we were to see our little homestead loom in the distance. We were not expected for another day, so had much trouble in rousing Berry and getting into our rooms. The storm came down with fury just after we were all under shelter, and continued all the next day.

So ended our first experience of a Round-up. The weather after this changed completely, and instead of the overpowering heat of the last week it was quite cold and wet, and I was not sorry to start for our long drive, after being boxed up for two days at the ranche. So we packed all our belongings once more on to the traps, leaving the tent behind, but in its place carrying a bag of corn in each trap between us. A very fat and heavy fellow passenger it was, but one that dwindled rapidly. The drive to Fort Robinson was excessively precipitous in places, and I marvel how anything on wheels managed to get down without overturning. I confess it took my breath away, so I got out at the worst places.

Fort Robinson was quite a big camp, with good houses and a store. Major Paddock came to welcome us very hospitably, and we stayed the night there. He gave us a most excellent dinner. The colonel and some of the officers called, and we had a very pleasant evening. The major was very proud of his dogs, and took me to see them. One was a half-bred Newfoundland and sheep dog—very good looking; the other I should be puzzled to class at all. We stayed the night at Fort Robinson, and it was delicious to sleep in a real bed with sheets once more.

We left our kind host early on the morning of the 13th June, as we had a long drive before us to Slate Springs, and right across the Bad Lands. Bad lands, truly—deep morasses. We had to wade through here and there a kind of ditch of thick black mud, which our gallant little horses half leapt and half plunged through. I drove in the buckboard with Mr. R——, and as we were the lightest we kept ahead bravely, till at one place we stuck fast, the horses above their hocks in mud, and the trap nearly sunk over the wheels.

Mr. R—— sprang out, but would not let me do so, and then endeavoured to cheer the little ponies through; but it was hopeless, we were fast. I climbed on to the pole and then sprang out on to firm ground. The corn bag was lugged off somehow, and then with a desperate effort that snapped our single tree like a twig, the good little horses managed to plunge out and stood panting and exhausted.

What a state we were all in, covered with thick black mud from head to foot; and this alkali mud is dreadful. It is more like putty, and marks for ever. We were all rather hungry after our efforts, so we decided to lunch where we were, and as we were doing so up rolled the stage coach and its six horses. They pulled up and the brakesman got down to examine the ground. Mr. R—— was going forward to warn them of our mishap, when the driver turned sharp off the track and drove right at what looked like a deep ditch. We all held our breath as we watched the proceeding. The horses plunged over, then the forewheels almost disappeared, the huge vehicle lurching like a ship in a storm. A storm of oaths and shouts from the driver, a cracking of whips, a bound, and somehow they were through and over, and driving gaily on as if nothing had happened at all unusual. But the passengers must have been black and blue, if, indeed, some of their bones were not dislocated. We passed a stage ranche further on, and the solitary horsekeeper told us this was the first coach through for eight days, owing to the state of the roads.

I will not weary my readers with any further description of our drive that day; suffice it to say we went from bad to worse. We stuck fast again and again, broke away the remains of our single tree, and this time the only available article to splice it with was poor J——'s boot jack. It almost broke his heart to see the useful old friend cut up, and how he was ever to remove his boots without it was a problem to be solved in the future. Poor Prince at last got quite out of heart, and took to jibbing at inopportune moments. We were devoured by the most blood-thirsty swarm of mosquitoes I ever felt, and our tempers waxed short, I fear. We were choked with mud and parched with thirst; but still we held on bravely. At about six o'clock we reached a solitary road ranche, and here we halted to feed and water the horses, and I went inside to make some tea. Two men were lying on the bed and did not trouble themselves to rise; but the stove was lighted and a big kettle puffed away, so I was able to make a good cup of tea without using my spirit lamp. The men looked on in a sort of quiet and surprised manner till the rest of the party came in, when they tumbled up and sat round talking. It was nearly dark now, and a wind blowing. After halting about thirty minutes we again drove on, and, as we were out of the Bad Lands, we were able to get along; but it did seem a weary, lonely drive truly, and it was quite one o'clock in the morning before we reached Slate Springs. And then it took us twenty minutes to knock up the owner, who quietly told us all the beds were full, but we might sleep on the floor of the parlour.

Can you imagine my feelings at hearing this? I was so very dead beat, with all we had gone through, that I did look forward to, at any rate, lying down outside a decent bed, and here we were all to be crammed in to this horrid stuffy parlour and to sleep on the boards. Well, there was no help for it, so while the men went with our good little horses to the stable to see that they, at any rate, were taken care of, I made my way into the kitchen, blew up the fire in the stove, and placed a big tin of ready-made coffee to heat. I then looked for something to eat, and found some biscuits and butter. As I was hunting about the owner of the place came in, having partly dressed, and condescended to help me. He laid the cloth as well as he could, and by the time the men came in I had hot coffee and dry toast ready; but we none of us felt inclined to eat much. I did not blow out my bed, it was too much trouble, so we unrolled the blankets and what wraps we had, and made ourselves as comfortable as we could.

In spite of my cruel weariness I could not sleep, and was glad when the morning broke. I crept up and out, and went to the stables. Seeing a well and a bucket I took the opportunity of having a refreshing wash in an out house, and felt much the better for it. I passed in to the stable and saw all the horses lying down comfortably. Then I went back, got our hardest clothes brush and endeavoured to get some of the mud off my skirt. I washed my boots, and, by degrees, made myself a little more presentable, and then a brilliant idea struck me, and I went into the kitchen, where I found two women busy making up the fire and preparing breakfast. I asked and obtained permission to carry out my brilliant idea, which was to make enough tea to fill a small barrel we had with us for water, but which we could not use as the water got so hot behind the buggy, and became anything but a refreshing drink. The women were going off by the stage to a ball somewhere, and were in a great state of excitement about it, so I was allowed to do as I liked. Finding a huge coffee pot, I proceeded to make my tea, tying the tea in a muslin bag and pouring boiling water upon it. I don't fancy I or anyone else would have thought it even drinkable at

home, but the time came when I coveted a mouthful
of the bitter stuff more than I ever longed for
anything in my life. Having filled the barrel and
corked it up, I made three good cups and carried it in
to the still sleeping partners of my journey, and very
pleased they were at such a delicate attention. By
now the people who were sleeping in the rooms began
to appear, as the stage was due in presently, and
after they had gone I looked into one or two of the
rooms, and they were so filthy that I don't think I
could have made up my mind to go to bed in any of
them.

After the stage left we got our breakfast, and made
a start as quickly as we could. We expected to have a
troublesome business crossing the Cheyenne River,
but, fortunately, it had run down, and though fairly
deep and strong it did not reach above the traces, and
the horses got a real good drink, poor things, and it
was all they did get, for there was no food for them
that morning, as we had to treasure the corn for
times when we should meet no ranches at all. It was a
red hot day, and a very dull drive through
uninteresting country.

About midday we halted at one of the very dirtiest
ranches I ever saw. An Irish bothy could not be
worse, and yet the occupiers were well-to-do folk,
with big cattle sheds and stables, and a good house;
they also kept a girl or help. Spite of the untidyness
of it all, we were thankful to get out of the scorching
sun and get a drink of milk. The people were very
hospitable, and got luncheon—such as it was—ready
for us at once, but we none of us cared about eating it,
it was all so dirty. The girl told me the daughters
were gone to the ball and would not be back for some

93

days, and she then described the dresses they wore, and gave us the impression that it was the great event of the year.

After giving the horses a good feed, and resting about an hour, we started again. The heat was dense, if I may use the word, till at last we heard the welcome growl of thunder, and in a few minutes we were in the midst of a furious storm, which cooled the air, laid the dust, and quite refreshed both man and beast. We were by this time driving through a very pretty country. Plenty of cotton trees, and a river was winding its way through the valley. Such lovely prairie flowers, and all as green as only the early spring can produce. We halted by the river and made tea, and I rambled some distance along its banks, enjoying the delicious air after the rain, and gathering a lovely bouquet of quite unknown (to me) wild flowers. I thoroughly enjoyed the drive that day. As our destination was only forty-five miles we went quite slowly, and we reached Battle Creek about 7 o'clock, where we found a charming ranche with a wide verandah running round it, and a garden, clean bedrooms, real beds with sheets on them, and, best of all, a bath. Having enjoyed the latter, we found a really good supper ready, served on a clean cloth, and such a pleasant neat little woman presiding at the table. I had a long chat with her afterwards, and made the acquaintance of the baby, and that night I slept as I had not done since we left Neobrara.

We had to reach Sturgeon City next day—some fifty odd miles off—so we made an early start. It was all pretty country, hilly and wooded in parts, and we passed a number of most curious volcanic formations like castles. The country reminded me much of Broxton, in Cheshire. The track also was quite plain.

We reached Rapid City about noon, and found it quite a big place. It had only been built recently. There was some sort of a civic ceremony going on, and the *table d'hôte* at the inn we put up at was crowded. I moved some chairs at one table close together to make room for us all, and by so doing roused the ire of the "young lady" who waited on us. She literally threw the dishes at us, and banged everything down in a manner that tested the quality of the delf; but when J——asked her to bring some beer she exploded, told him to fetch it himself, and marched off, declining to wait on us any further, to the intense amusement of the other people at our table, who, no doubt, thought she showed a proper spirit to us darned Englishers. I was very tired and burnt up, and went up stairs to rest in a sort of sitting room, but, unfortunately, I found a man and his wife there with a dot of a child of about three, to whom they were most anxious to teach the America habit of spitting, and the noises they made and the horridness of the whole thing so disgusted me that I took refuge in the passage till we started again, which we shortly did. We found the roads very bad for our next stage, and had to be careful of our splinter bar, as it was only held together by the pieces of boot jack and straps. We passed a number of bull teams, and at one very steep place had to drive off the track on to the hill side to pass one of them. J—— and Mr. B—— jolted together to the side lowest down, and at once the buggy over-balanced, rolled completely over, and threw them under the feet of the team, to my horror. I was looking back and saw them. Poor Mr. B—— was hurt, but J—— escaped all safe. The strange part of the whole business was that when the buggy was lifted up and put on its wheels the luggage was all

there. It had never stirred. Of course, we laughed
very much over the incident when we found no
serious harm had been done. We stayed that night at
a small inn, a wretched place, but freshly white-
washed all over, so that it was clean, at all events. I
sat out on the flat roof till quite late, and then lay
down on the bed, but there were beasts that bit, so
that it was a very bad night for me.

Sturgeon City is quite a big place, with a post office
and telegraph station, and some stores. The country
about was quite pretty, rather like Lowland Scotland, with fir trees and hills, and it was a very pretty
drive to Spearfish. We crossed Blood River, which
quite deserves its name, as it runs down as red as
blood. Deadwood City is on it, a mining centre of
some importance. It was only about twenty miles on
to Spearfish, and we drove up to Overland House
about one o'clock; but, fortunately, it was full, so we
went on to Roque's Hotel, where rooms were taken
for us by Mrs. R——, who, with her daughter and son,
a clergyman, were living at Spearfish. I say
fortunately, as we found out afterwards that Roque's
was far and away the most comfortable place. I had a
nice room opening on to a verandah, with three
windows, white curtained beds and an armchair, as
well as a clean carpet; and it was quite a treat, after
our rough life, to sit down on a chair at all. There
were capital bath rooms, and I at once indulged in the
luxury of a bathe, and when dressed in clean things
and a cotton print dress felt more like my old self
than I had done for a long time. All our letters were
waiting here for us. Such a budget of home news, and
no bad tidings amongst it; the dogs all well, sending
their love, according to Elizabeth! and everything

apparently going smoothly across the water. Presently, Mr. R—— entered, looking a civilised being again—washed, dressed, shaved, and neat as a new pin. He brought me a tray of cakes and sweetmeats from his mother and a whole lot of tinned fruits, a kind of "welcome" offering to their town. The only drawback was, that a very important letter which he expected from Mr. Hewitt had, in some mysterious manner, got delayed, and this was very annoying, as it might cause us all delay. Mr. R—— wired at once to endeavour to obtain some tidings respecting it.

The *table d'hôte* at Roque's was as primitive as it well could be. The hostler and two men-helps sat at the table next to ours, but they were quite well conducted—indeed, more so than some of the people I have met at smarter hotels. It was very, very hot all day and my head ached dreadfully, so, after unpacking our few belongings and putting the room more to my fancy, I did not go out. Old Mrs. R—— and her daughter came to call after dinner, and I made them some tea on the balcony. Mrs. R—— quite appreciated its superiority to their own. She was a very pleasant old lady, a perfect type of the Old England American school, and a rigid Puritan. Her daughter, a very pretty girl, was engaged to a Mr. Millar, a very enterprising Scotchman we met there, who owned a flourishing horse ranche. As we were sitting at tea a loud clap of thunder startled us, and by-and-bye down came the rain. The storm did not last long, and left the air cool and fresh. We stayed a few days at Spearfish to rest the horses, get our clothes washed and wait for the eagerly-wished-for letter, but it never turned up, and eventually we had to leave without it. I rode a good deal and we made some expeditions to the environs. I also attended service in the little school house; such a pleasant Scotch service it was. Mr. R——'s brother was the parson of Spearfish, and had done a great deal to civilise the people since he came there. It must have been a dreadfully rough place before his advent. We went to an evening entertainment at Mrs. R——'s rooms and met quite the prettiest American girl I ever saw, a Daisy Miller to the life. She played the banjo and sang to it, and all her pretty ways and little conquetries seemed so out of place amongst the rough folks. One of the party came in a flannel shirt and no coat; and to see this pretty delicate creature in white muslin and blue ribbons certainly was not one of the least strange anomalies I have witnessed.

I was very glad to start once more on our travels, as many things vexed me in Spearfish. There was a horse-breaker who was always cruelly ill-treating one unfortunate pony, apparently for no reason. One day the unhappy brute literally lay down and remained as if dead. Finding that kicks in its ribs produced no effect he then took the butt end of his whip and struck it repeatedly just behind its ears. At the fifth blow I rushed to the rescue, but it had sprung up and was going round as if in great pain, and before I could get to him (not that I could have done any good) the brutal owner had mounted it and was spurring and flogging it cruelly, going at a hard gallop out of the town. Then a poor dog had come in lost, a big yellow kind of greyhound, and everyone vied with each other in ill-treating it, poor beast! At last some brutes tied an old pot to its tail and began to pelt it. J——, at this, could stand it no longer, but "went" for them. The poor beast was too terrified to run, and allowed me to untie the pot. I think the men

were a little ashamed of themselves. This sort of
thing affects me painfully, especially when one is so
helpless to do anything to stop it.

It was brilliant weather when we started, but we
had a very rough road. Messrs. B—— and R—— were
to follow, and the old lady with her son drove the
buggy with the buckskins, and a nice mess they
made of it, driving into a boghole before we were four
miles clear of the town, and in extricating the trap
poor Charlie got a badly galled shoulder. When we
reached Sun Dance, where we were to sleep, they
drove on some five miles to call at a ranche. I was
very angry, especially as we had to do up the horses
for ourselves, and wanted to give them as long a
night as possible. Sun Dance was a filthy den, and I
declined to sleep in the place we "ladies" were given,
a sort of outhouse where fleeces and general rubbish
were stored away, and I dragged my buffalo robe and
blankets outside, where it was fresh, and a dear old
colley came and snuggled down by me all night and
kept me warm.

Next morning Charlie's shoulder was too sore for
him to bear his collar, and we tied him behind the
buggy, and put in an old horse Mr. R—— was taking
for riding. Then we found our little mare had hurt
her fore leg, and it was much swollen; and when I
took her down to water she was very stiff. As there
was a lovely quick-running brook, I made her stand
in it, and bathed her fore leg with my sponge for half
an hour, which seemed to do the damaged leg great
good. She was such a gentle, kind little creature, and
very sensible, for I could plainly see she quite knew I
was trying to help her. I don't think any of our
journeys was such a weary one as this, the track was
so stony, we had to go up and down such steep places,

and it was so hot with not a breath of air. We halted for luncheon at a very desolate spot; not a vestige of shade to be found; but there was water for the poor horses, and I was able to bathe the little mare's leg again. She had quite walked off her lameness, strange to say; but going down hill she kept hitting the bad place.

Miss R—— and Mr. Millar, who were riding, were able to make a much shorter cut than we could, and, indeed, I often found myself wishing for a horse to ride, as it would have saved me such a lot of shaking when we came to the very rough places. I felt really dead beat, and was thankful when, at about five o'clock, we reached Belle Fourche, Mr. R——'s own little ranche. There was no one there, except the cook; of course, he could not dream of helping us to unload or see to the horses, so we had to do the best we could for ourselves. J—— got a pail of warm water to wash the thick casing of mud off the mare's sore leg, and I made a bandage for it out of a woollen stocking, having first rubbed it well with some grease, and we made her a good bed in the shed. I saw she ate well, and was pleased. Before we could get all our luggage off the buckboard, a loud thunder clap warned us to hurry, and in a few moments down came the rain in such torrents we were thankful to have a roof over our heads.

This ranche was a very good one. There was a large sleeping room, and a dining room, besides the kitchen, together with several places like outhouses, so that we were able to make our arrangements for the night independently of each other. We were presently called to supper, and I confess I was surprised at the little trouble that had been taken to bring something decent to eat, as it would have been so easy to have sent over from Spearfish, with the cook, meat and groceries; but I think the Americans pride themselves rather on not making things comfortable, so as to enhance the "roughing." Our supper consisted of badly cooked potatoes, heavy rolls of fat bacon, and as I could not get accustomed to eat this kind of food I did not fare too sumptuously. Fortunately, there was a cow, so milk was plentiful, and the coffee fairly good. The storm was soon over; but the ground was so saturated with rain that it was just a bed of soft mud, and we turned in early—I slept on the air bed on the dining room table.

About two o'clock a loud cracking of whips and shouts told us Mr. R—— and B—— had arrived, greatly to our surprise, as they were not expected till the next evening. They had made a forced march, and run the two days' journey into one, driving over sixty miles with a pair of young and very wild horses just up from grass. They had had no end of mishaps, as they got off the trail in the dark and stuck in a creek for some time, breaking the single trees in getting out. One of their horses took to lying down, and, altogether, I felt thankful they arrived without any bones broken. The next day was one of real rest, and looking to the horses. Charlie's shoulder was better, as the large lump on it had burst, and the little mare's leg was nearly well. We lounged about in the shade all day, and towards evening Mr. Millar rode over to propose our going out after an antelope. There was such an ominous black horizon, J—— thought I had better not go, and lucky it was, as after they started we had the most fearful storm, accompanied with thunder and lightning. I had never, even in the tropics, seen anything like it. The rain came down in sheets, flooding the kitchen and dining room, and nearly floating the men's beds out. The ground outside became a simple swamp, and when the poor hunters got back they were as wet as if they had swum through a river. It took us nearly all night to get their things even fairly dried, and we had to be off in good time next morning.

Fortunately, it was quite clear again, and very hot; but the river was so high, it was rather difficult to ford it. I made a whole barrel of tea before we started, as we should find nothing but alkali springs for the greater part of the journey, and Mrs. R—— had made us a cake. We also took a bottle of milk for our luncheon. The country here was exceedingly pretty, very like driving over Welsh moors, except that here and there cotton trees were growing by the creek sides, and, instead of heather, such rich grass. We here again remarked the apparent scarcity of stock. It was really remarkable how very few herds of cattle we saw all through our drive. The day was very threatening, and we saw a large waterspout in the distance, which did not raise our spirits, as we knew this meant finding the creeks overflowing, heavy going, and damp sleeping places.

We reached MacCraig's Ranche about six o'clock. Our approach was notified by the loud barking of dogs, and some six or eight very peculiar but remarkably good looking sheep dogs came bounding to meet us. They were rather like the bob-tailed colley breed, only with tails and more silky coats, but such lovely heads, all black and white. One old patriarch came up to me very gravely and, having satisfied himself I was a friend, followed me into the house. Mr. MacCraig was hospitality itself, but it was a perfect den of a place, consisting of two rooms, one the kitchen, one the sleeping room. The heavy

rain had softened the mud flooring, which stuck to
our boots. Outside, the water was some inches deep
everywhere, as the waterspout had burst somewhere
in this neighbourhood. A supper was prepared to
which we all sat down together, master and men, but
I could not eat, and afterwards I stood in the doorway
looking out at the very damp prospect, and feeling,
for the first time, that there were limits to one's
appreciation of "roughing" it. Mr. MacCraig and his
men seemed very happy. They sat smoking and
spitting all over the floor, talking very big about
some hunt they had been at, till bedtime. The master
kindly intimated that I was to have his bed and he
would sleep with his men, and he rigged up a kind of
screen with some old blankets, but it was no use—I
could not (no, I could not) make up my mind to lie
down on it. So I went into the kitchen, under pretence
of washing my hands, and remained till they were all
asleep, Mr. B—— and R—— on their rugs on the
floor, J—— on my bed, and the other two in a bunk in
the wall, when I crept in and rolled my bundle of
bedding near the fire, and sat on it till welcome dawn
made its appearance. Quite the most weary night I
ever spent.

I don't fancy any of us had rested much, as the
mosquitoes were very troublesome, and this, no
doubt, affected our tempers a little, as the first and
only disagreement that occurred throughout our
journey took place between two of us here. I won't say
any more about this, as it was after all a very
short-lived affair, and not altogether unreasonable
under the circumstances. I felt very fagged and worn
out, and glad to get on. Mr. MacCraig looked very
coldly on me, I thought, and, indeed, I heard long
afterwards that he could not forgive my refusing his

bed, and called me "a darned stuck-up Englisher."
He rode for a few miles to put us in the right road, and
then we drove along a flat stony track for some way,
till suddenly there loomed in front a silver streak,
which widened as we gained the banks, and, lo! the
Wild Cat Creek, now a rushing, broad river, the
water almost level to its banks, presented a truly
formidable obstacle. We took counsel among ourselves, but it was really a choice of evils. Either we
must go back to MacCraig's, and wait a day or so for
the water to run down, or swim the creek bag and
baggage. I think we were all agreed, and Mr. R——
was to make the trial trip with the buggy, I only
stipulating that he must come back to take the
buckboard over. He had swum rivers in buggies
before, whereas we were ignorant of the first
principles of the thing. J—— would swim across as
soon as they were safe on the other side.

It was a moment of intense excitement, but the
good buckskins walked calmly to the very brink, and
then half slipped, half bucked into the stream. In a
second they were out of their depth, and swimming
steadily for the opposite shore. Was the landing
sound? Yes. There was a struggle, a scramble, and
they were all standing on dry land, the water pouring
out of the buggy in a stream, everything, of course,
drenched. Mr. R—— lost no time, but got unloaded as
quickly as possible, and shouted to us that instead of
swimming back and bringing me over in the
buckboard, he would bring the buggy back, and could
follow with the little horses—an unlucky idea as it
turned out. Seeing what looked like a better landing
a few yards higher up, he made for it, but it was a
mistake. True, the bank was not nearly so steep, but
there was no foothold; it was a mud hole. Poor

Charlie and Frank stuck; finding themselves sinking they struggled frantically. J—— and I tried to pacify them all we knew. The strong current caught the buggy and over it went, throwing Mr. R—— into the water. I should mention that in anticipation of such an event he had taken off everything to his underclothing. He was carried a long way down the stream before Mr. B—— could throw off his coat and, plunging gallantly in, come to our rescue. I held on to poor Charlie's head like grim death. The horses had ceased struggling and now lay like logs, and it was all we could do to keep the poor brutes above water. Meanwhile the two men in the water were doing their best to unfasten the traces, but the strain was so great it was all but impossible, and Mr. R—— would not listen to the suggestion to unfasten the collars and so free the whole thing, as he feared we might lose the harness in the strong current.

It seemed ages, but no doubt was only a few minutes, before the last trace was freed; then the buggy, rolling over and over, sailed gaily down the torrent, but, fortunately, struck on a sand bank in the middle of the river, and, strange to say, righted itself. We were now able to give all our attention to saving the horses. The first thing was to get them to move, so we pushed and pulled them back into the stream, so as to be in deep water again, and then got them to the bank a little lower down, where there was a footing. They were so frightened that it was some time before they would try. At last, with a frantic struggle, Charlie scrambled on land, knocking me over and trampling on me, as I would not leave go of him, fearing that he would make a bolt of it; then Frank pulled himself together for a mighty effort, and stood panting and heaving on the bank. I think the relief of mind at having them once more safe and sound on *terra firma* outdid the agony we all went through. It is no uncommon thing to lose a horse in accidents of this kind, and both the buckskins were so precious.

Having securely fastened them behind the buckboard, we now had to turn our attention to the buggy. Mr. R—— swam over for the rope we fastened our luggage with, and tied it firmly to the splinter-bars, and then we all pulled and tugged. Oh! how I tugged, but to no purpose; it was too firmly lodged. We then fastened Frank to it, but this was no use. At last we managed to get it tied on to the back of the buckboard, and then, uniting all our efforts to those of the ponies, we had the satisfaction of feeling it move; it floated and finally was dragged in triumph on to the bank, and not a spoke injured—on the contrary, the good sousing it had had had washed off all the accumulation of alkali mud from wheels and body, and it looked quite clean and bright again. There was no time to lose, however, so, after a hasty examination, the horses' harness was readjusted, the buckboard seen to, and then Mr. R—— took his seat and drove the little ponies to the brink. At first they looked like refusing, but only for a moment, then in they plunged, and in a few moments were scrambling up the other side.

Now came my turn. I took off my skirt and boots and stockings, and put on my waterproof. J—— divested himself of his upper garments and swam lower down the creek, so as to catch me if I got thrown out. I knelt on the seat to keep as much above the water as I could, shut my eyes for an instant as we made the plunge off the bank, and truly delicious it was to feel the cool grateful water creeping up around me. The gallant buckskins never even hesitated, but, in spite of their late terrible experience, breasted the waves gallantly, and then we were all safe across, but wringing wet, and everything we had with us in a similar condition. We at once unhitched and gave the horses their food. Then we each unpacked our own luggage and laid everything out in the sun. It looked exactly like a drying ground, but the heat that day was really terrible, the sun baking down on our heads, and in less than an hour everything was quite dry.

I lay down under the waggon, as the sun really seemed to scorch my brains, and I fell into an exhausted sleep, an example which all soon followed.

Thus ended the only real mishap that we met with all through our rough drive.

We did not move till about four in the afternoon, when we had a hasty meal and drank some more cold tea, which, by the way, we had greedily swallowed as soon as I could get it fairly cool, which I did by tying the rope to it and throwing it into the river. It had remained tied behind the buckboard in the sun, and was nearly scalding hot. We all felt pretty well done up, I think. I know I did, and no great wonder, considering how I had passed the night at Mac-Craig's Ranche. We were driving sleepily along, when a shout from Mr. R—— aroused us. He was gesticulating wildly for us to stop, which we did, and only in time, as not a couple of yards off, right in our path, a hideous rattlesnake lay coiled ready to spring; the buggy must have driven over it, but by great good fortune it had not had time to strike. Mr. R—— came with his whip and struck with all his might (these creatures are very easily killed if struck with a pliable weapon). He then took out the rattle, which I have to this day, and we continued on our way. The sun was going down as we sighted Mr. Richie's ranche. Mr. Richie is a Scotch rancheman, with such a kind, cheery little Canadian wife. They knew Mr. R—— quite well, and came out to welcome and help us. The house was so neat and nice, their own room being prettily papered and hung with little white curtains at the windows. But the house was only half built then. The stables were also very good, and our horses were in clover for once. After a very well-cooked and nicely-served supper of beef, potatoes, and a kind of hasty pudding, which I thoroughly enjoyed, we got out our beds and bedding and I put them outside, as we would not intrude on Mr. Richie's privacy, and presently, regardless of the mosquitoes, we enjoyed our well-earned rest.

Next day Mr. Richie organised a buffalo hunt for us and provided us each with a mount, all but Mr. R——, who preferred a quiet day. We had a delightful ride over the hills, and it reminded me again of North Wales. The pasturage was splendid in the valley near the creek, the grass standing as high as an average English hayfield. We rode for some hours, but saw no buffaloes; at length we discerned a fine antelope standing on the hill side, some three hundred yards off. J—— and Mr. B—— dismounted and began to stalk him, whilst we stood holding the horses in breathless expectation. J—— fired first, but though we saw the stones fly apparently at the antelope's very feet, he never stirred. Mr. B—— then blazed away, but to no purpose, and then, and then only, did he trot quietly off, looking back as he gained the hill top as if in contempt of his assailants. I was heartily glad to see him escape unharmed. We then returned to the ranche, and after an excellent

luncheon of cold beef and potatoes bade our
hospitable hosts adieu, wondering if we should ever
meet again. The poor little woman died nearly a year
after, and the ranche failed and Mr. Richie had to
leave. They had two little children, a boy and a girl,
and I pitied the little boy very much, his father was so
harsh to him. He was a high-spirited little fellow,
only about five years of age, and always in mischief. I
misdoubt me, when the poor mother died that child's
life would be but a sad one. However, this is a
digression.

We drove off through the splendid long grass (I
never saw such a grass country as this) till we had to
leave the valley and take to the uplands, and then
the road really became dangerous. We were making
for the Little Powder River, and should, we since
learnt, have taken a trail a good deal higher up.
Instead, we soon found ourselves in a series of what I
can only call miniature divides—precipitate steeps
to drive down, a small stream generally running at
the bottom, to be leapt or scrambled over, and a bank
like a house side to climb. On horse back it would
have been uneasy work enough, but on wheels it
looked really like madness to attempt it. Of course,
Mr. B—— and I got out to lighten the trap as much as
possible. I felt horribly nervous, but J—— drove
grandly. Of course, Mr. R—— was more used to it. To
give my readers an idea of the width of the streams,
or, rather, mud holes, we came to one that
necessitated a good run at it. I jumped as far as I
could, but landed on a treacherous spot, and had Mr.
B—— not grabbed me by the arm I should have had
the most disagreeable black mud bath in the world.
Our little horses had to jump these, dragging the
traps after them as they best could. How the wheels

stood it I don't know. We carried all the loose things, such as bags, cushions, the tea-bottle, &c., otherwise everything would have been sent flying. I was very thankful when, after a wider and steeper divide than ever, Mr. R—— sighted the track we were in search of, and once more we were driving over a comparatively smooth road.

The sun was setting in crimson and gold, the Little Powder River looked like a silver streak, and the lovely colouring of the hills as a background and the vivid green of the long grass we were then driving through made a picture of prairie scenery as wild and beautiful as it was possible to imagine. Hundreds of flowers were blooming all around, and some of the largest and most beautiful butterflies I ever saw were flitting about. I should have dearly liked to linger a little in such a paradise, but we were making for a certain point, and were very late. We passed a bunch of cattle and some cowboys on their way towards Spearfish, and further on some more were being driven into a species of kraal for the night. We had now left the luxuriant pasture land and were driving over short scrub that in the gathering dusk might be mistaken for heather. As to track or trail, there was none. At last, so dark did it get that J—— and I could only follow the other trap by calling constantly after them, "Where are you? Which way?" All at once a dismal yell in front of us of "Keep back; for Heaven's sake stop!" made us pull up abruptly, my heart in my mouth, as I thought for an instant they had gone down some chasm. We sprang out and ran forward, to see a most laughable spectacle. The buggy had suddenly been swung over a dry mud creek, the horses having jumped it suddenly. Mr. R—— was struggling up from under their feet, or, rather, from off Charlie's back, where he had been precipitated, and Mr. B——'s head was just discernible as he crept out of the ditch. Their fear was lest we should have come on top of them, when dire would have been the mischief. All's well that ends so, and we could not help laughing over the absurdity of it all. The difficulty was to find the path again, as we had quite gone astray. Mr. R—— struck matches and we groped about till, more by good luck than good judgment, we managed to strike it and drove on.

The moon had risen, so we got on well for some miles, till at last the Little Powder River stopped our further progress. Mr. R—— was all for our trying to cross it and pushing on to Number One Ranche, but this we all were emphatically against, as after our experience at the Wild Cat Creek we did not care to risk a wetting at night. Mr. R—— unharnessed Charlie and rode him across. He did not actually swim, but was as nearly doing so as he could. *Ergo*, the traps would have been over their wheels in the water; so that settled the matter, and we prepared to bivouac by the stream under the cotton trees. The horses were unharnessed and turned loose to graze; the only precaution we took to prevent them straying was to hobble the little mare. Then we all separated to collect dry wood, and presently had a grand fire blazing. Our supper was but a poor one, as we had only a tin of cold trout, some crackers (very few of these) and the tea, which this time I contrived to make in an empty fruit tin. Of course, we ought to have brought a coffee-pot and coffee with us, also corned beef or some kind of eatable, but Mr. R—— had undertaken to run the whole concern, and it was out of our hands. But it was a pity, as in addition to hard days and bad nights, we really at times had not

111

enough to eat, unless we came across a road ranche and got some beef and bread. However, we made the best of it, drank our milkless, sugarless tea, crunched our biscuits, and then rolled ourselves up and lay down to rest.

Sleep I could not; it was all so strange, lovely and weird—the white cotton trees standing like spectres in the bright moonlight, the black river splashing slowly by, the fire throwing out strange gleams, the mournful cry of the coyote in the distance, and the shrill cry of some nightbird and the swish of its wings as it flew past—it was a scene I longed to be able to put on canvas, a scene never to be forgotten. At last, unable to keep still any longer, I rose, and in my slippers walked noiselessly to the edge of the cotton tree clump and looked over the wide expanse. My thoughts flew home, and I wondered what all were doing. How strange if they could picture to themselves my exact whereabouts! I was getting quite romantic and melancholy, when, ugh! I trod suddenly on some soft substance that began to struggle and squirm under my foot. How I jumped back! I thought of a rattlesnake. I heard it scramble off amongst the dried leaves and grass, and I hurried back to the fire light and my air bed quite cured of any further wish for a ramble by moonlight.

We were off betimes next morning; the river had run down considerably, so we escaped a wetting. We passed the Number One Ranche, but found it deserted. I felt very glad indeed that we had not pushed on there the night before; it was a horrid little place, a mere hut, frightfully dirty and infested with swarms of black flies. There was a good spring of water, so we filled our barrel, as the tea had come to an end. We met the Round-up some miles further on, encamped with the waggons under a little wood of cotton trees by the river. The men were soon mounted and off to where the branding was going on; I longed to have a horse and go with them, but as no one seemed to think this was advisable I remained grilling under the trees the live-long day; and a weary day it was. From time to time a cowboy, heated and dirty, rode in to snatch a mouthful of food and change his horse. I talked with the cook, rather a fine old fellow, and mended some of the garments that had got torn during our travels, but was sincerely glad when, about six, my own belongings rode in, dead beat and covered with dust. They had all been hard at work branding and driving. Mr. B—— had carried a little motherless calf before him for a long distance. They all seemed to think I had had by far the best of it. We made a hasty meal of a bit of tough cold beef and some bread, and started for Mr. Smith's ranche, where we were to sleep—a delicious drive in the cool air, through pretty, undulating country. We passed numbers of cattle and cowboys all making towards the Round-up we had just left, and a few bunches setting off towards the nearest railway for shipment. Wonderfully well they all looked, so fat and sleek.

We found a solitary and consumptive lad in charge of Smith's ranche. Poor boy! he had come out West in the hope that it might do him good, but the lonely life and bad food seemed to have counteracted any good the climate might have effected, and he looked terribly bad. He told me we were the first people he had seen to talk to for six weeks, and I was the first woman he had seen for over six months. He did his best to make us comfortable, but bad potatoes and worse coffee were all he had to offer us. We were too tired to care about eating. I had my bed in the kitchen on the table, but waited till all were asleep and then contrived to have a hot bath, having unpacked our india-rubber tub and boiled a big kettle of water on the stove. It was most refreshing, and I felt a new person. The heat was suffocating, so eventually I carried my bed and blankets outside and had a really good night's rest, a luxury I had not enjoyed since we left Spearfish. After a breakfast similar to our supper we got off in good time and had the misfortune to leave one of our slickers* behind; fortunately we had lovely weather the rest of the time.

Our route was a very circuitous one, and ten times we had to cross the Little Powder—getting our baggage all wet, and losing our keg of water and the boot-jack, which were carried rapidly down. A sand bank in the middle stranded them, so we regained their possession. I forgot to say that Mr. MacCraig's men had made J—— a capital boot-jack out of a strong box lid, to replace the one we had cut up. There was no trail now, as we were in a very unfrequented part of the prairie. Such lovely flowers were growing, and at one place we drove through and over a perfect thicket of wild roses; the scent was delicious, like attar of roses, and very strong. We halted at Mr. Ferdan's new ranche. Two men were building it; at least they were holding the place till Mr. Ferdan came over to settle the spot. They shared their supper with us, or we should have had very short commons; and we also had the advantage of their camp fire. The horses revelled in a perfect

---

*A "slicker is a waterproof coat.

paradise of grass, and as a part was fenced off they were quite free to roam as they liked unhobbled.

When I awoke about five the next morning we were enshrouded in a thick white mist. It was not possible to see any object a couple of yards away. This was a most curious phenomenon, as the white, curtain-like fog was only about a yard high. Everything was heavy with moisture—our blankets saturated, except where covered with the mackintosh sheets. The sun was rising, and seemed to soak up the mist like a cloud. I never saw so curious a sight, though, of course, it is a quite usual occurrence on a flat, marshy piece of land near a river. We had a good cup of coffee and some bread and bacon, and got off about six. We should have forded the Big Powder River and so got on the coach road, but we found this impossible. The snow from the Rockies was melting, and the river was running flush with the banks and very strong. It was not a case of Wild Cat Creek, as it was as wide as three Wild Cats, and we had to make our way over a mountain trail that was but seldom used.

All we had hitherto done was child's play to this day's work. Mr. R—— walked in front to find a feasible path up the steep precipitate face of the hill, J—— drove one trap, Mr. B—— another, and I scrambled behind with big stones to place behind the wheels. Of course, though very steep, the climb was short, or the horses could not have done it. Even as it was, when, on reaching the top of the first hill, we could see where we were, I certainly despaired of our ever driving over such a country. Sharp abrupt declines, and again as sharp rises over a line of volcanic hills, here and there impassable precipices—these we had to skirt till we were able to find a descent. At last we got to a narrow ledge, just wide enough for the wheels and no more, and no possibility of turning back; we had to go on. Mr. R—— got into the buggy and started on the forlorn hope. It was an anxious moment, as had one of the horses jibbed or shied they were done for; but they never hesitated. Straining in their traces they gallantly breasted the steep and rugged hill, and at last, panting and breathless, they gained the top. Then came J—— with the ponies, and my heart stood still. If Prince showed temper when it came to the sharp turn what would happen? J—— stood up, and encouraging them with voice and hands they started with a dash. Brave little beasts! slipping and scrambling over the loose stones they never gave way, and in even less time than the buckskins took they also were standing on the summit. And now it was an almost continuous descent for the rest of the way. I was thankful to be well out of this difficulty without mishap, but the going was still so rough, and unlike my ideas of what was drivable, that I still preferred keeping on my feet. As the horses could only go at a slow pace, with constant rests, this did not delay us. The heat was tropical, and thankful I was when at last, after quite the roughest and hardest scramble I had ever had, we did reach the stage coach trail. It had taken us six hours to get so far, and the horses were more done up than they had ever been in a day's work.

We got along well till we sighted the Big Powder again, and here we had to cross it somehow. We drove up to a good-sized ranche that was kept by the man who was to show us the practicable fording place, but soon found he was not "at home." However, this made no difference. The horses were taken out and led under a shed to be out of the broiling sun and get a little cooled down before we could water them, then we made a tour of inspection of the ranche. It was a quaint place, larger than a road ranche usually is. Two rooms, divided by a wide space, roofed over so as to give shade in the hottest hours of the day, and in the middle was a well and a bucket. This was truly a welcome sight. We had not tasted a drop of fresh or even cool water for days, and on drawing some up it proved not only icy cold but deliciously free of alkali. How we drank! I fear we never stopped to consider the wisdom of such a proceeding—tumbler after tumbler, and still we could not assuage our thirst. We were still busy drawing water for the horses into my india-rubber foot-pan, when the owner of the ranche arrived. He was greatly surprised to learn the road we had come, and seemed to think it a very wild proceeding, and greatly marvelled at "a lady" travelling such a rough road. Later on he informed Mr. R—— that if all English women were as strong as I was they must be a fine race, as I seemed a real "Rustler." This, I believe, is a term of approval.

The little man was very hospitable, and brought out the best he had—coffee, bread and some dried buffalo tongue—really very good, but I could not eat much; indeed, my thirst was still so great I could not assuage it. I have no doubt now that I laid the foundation of a very serious illness I endured going home, at that same sparkling well of ice-cold water.

We rested for a good couple of hours till the great heat had a little abated, and then drove down to the river side. It looked pretty bad, running very strong and sluggishly, but full to the banks and steadily rising. Fording it was quite out of the question, so we had to take the wheels off the traps so as to ferry them over in the boat. Mr. R—— and I crossed over at once with the bags and baggage, and I sat watching from the other side as there was a little shade under the high banks.

The trouble was, how to get the horses over. At first Mr. R—— tried swimming them behind the boat, but the current was so strong the boat kept drifting down and the horses twice broke away. Once, Charlie nearly came across, but got stuck on a sand bank, and we were terrified lest he should get so fast in the mud that he would be drowned. He did get off at last, but landed on the wrong side again. After several fruitless efforts Mr. R—— decided to swim them over, and this he managed capitally—riding Charlie and leading Frank—and as soon as the good sensible creatures felt they had their friend and master near them they seemed to lose all fear, walked gently till out of their depth and then swam to the other side like lambs. I was there to receive them, and at once took them off to the road ranche, about half-a-mile off, when I got them into the stable, and after hunting up the proprietor had soon the pleasure of seeing them enjoying a real good feed of corn and as much hay as they cared for. I then hurried back to bring on the little ones, who I found had crossed just as sensibly.

On my second journey to the ranche I went in to ask for some water, and to my great delight the woman of the place brought me a delicious jug of milk with big lumps of ice in it. This I carried back to our landing place and shared with Mr. B——, who had just brought over the last boat load of our goods and chattels preparatory to bringing over the traps. My

poor feet were so sore and burning by this time, what
with the long, hot climb over the mountain, and alas!
I had trod on a cactus, and one of the thorns had gone
clean through the sole of my thick field boots, but this
was early in the day, and, thanks to Mr. B——, I had
got it extracted at once. Still the wound it made was
very painful, and I felt a longing to bathe my feet in
the fast-running river, so taking off boots and
stockings I sat on the edge and plunged them in to
the stream. It was quite warm, I found—at least, not
at all cold; and thinking I should find a cooler place if
I got out of the sun round a bend, I began cautiously
to walk along in the water up to my knees. I had not
gone six yards when, without warning of any kind, I
slipped into a deep hole quite overhead. As I felt
myself sinking I instinctively clutched towards the
bank and grasped, entirely by accident, a slender
willow stem that was in the stream.

I had heard that when drowning all the past life of
the victim runs through his brain, and I can quite
believe it. As I floated with only this slender twig
between me and death (for, even could they have
heard my cries it was impossible that any boat could
have crossed in time to save me) thoughts of home
and the loved ones left there, and of many little
events never remembered before, flitted through my
mind, and chiefly I felt so sorry for J—— when he
should find out what a terrible calamity had befallen
me. I did not struggle or fight, but merely held on to
my willow wand, and the current running strong
enough to have washed Charlie back from the bank
had now changed, and I felt sucked under as it were,
and so was able to grasp another twig, and then
another, and then, feeling it was strong enough, I

drew myself close to shore, and grasped the trunk of
the willow, and thankfully crawled on to the bank,
where I lay for a few minutes drenched and exhausted, but, oh! how thankful to feel once more on
the dry, hard ground. Had I not caught the bough I
must have been washed swiftly down; and the worst
part would have been that no one would have found
out anything till hours after. Our men were all too
busy with the waggons, first taking off the wheels
and ferrying the traps across one by one, and then
putting the wheels back—a most tedious job; and
when this was done it was getting well on in the
afternoon. They would have imagined that, tired
with sitting in the sun waiting, I had gone to the
ranche to rest, and it would only have dawned upon
them that something was wrong when they came
over to bring the horses back to the traps and found I
had not been seen. The only evidence to show what
had happened would have been the boots and
stockings waiting on the bank for feet that never
again would have needed them; and as to when the
poor body would have been found who can tell—
probably never! It was a merciful escape, and I felt
thankful to kind Providence for my rescue.

The sun was so hot that my outer garments soon
dried, even without taking them off, and I was so
exhausted I lay down in the sun, sheltered under my
umbrella, and fell into a dead sleep for over an hour,
and by then the buckboard was across, and J—— and
I set to to put on the wheels. I did not mention my
mishap, as I felt rather ashamed of myself for
allowing it to occur. It was weary work getting the
wheels screwed on, and the men were black with
heat. At last it was accomplished, and we all walked

to the ranche and got some bread, butter and milk, and, to the great delight of J—— and Mr. B——, some fairly good bottled beer. This really did us all a lot of good. We were nearly worn out for want of decent food, and the beer gave a stimulus greatly needed.

We carried off a bottle of milk and one of beer, and some bread, and then, just as the sun was beginning to set, we started for the road ranche we meant to sleep at some twenty-two miles further on. Such a delicious evening it was after the scorching heat, and the luxury of a defined road instead of always having to look for a trail was very resting. True, the road was very bad and steep, and we bumped and jumped over wide crevices that in the dusk we hardly saw; but the horses were thoroughly refreshed by their good meal and rest, and trotted merrily away. It was quite dark when we reached the ranche, a poor one-roomed place, and as we found two men in possession, one of whom was down with some kind of fever, we made our arrangements for sleeping out as usual. There were two empty mule waggons standing by, so we spread our rugs and blankets in these; I did not trouble about the air bed, it was such a business blowing it out.

No supper could be got at the ranche as the stove was out, so I opened our bottle of milk and found it of the consistency of a stiff jelly—quite sour. However, Mr. R—— and I did not find it bad eaten with a bit of bread. The other two shared the bottle of beer. The night was very cold, strange to say, and a heavy dew or white mist enveloped everything. My clothes were more than damp, and I woke up shivering violently and feeling as if I should soon be very ill. However, I rolled my fur cloak well round me and by degrees got warm; but next morning I felt stiff and weary for the first time during our long journey.

Our horses had been let loose without any hobbling, only Charlie had a long rope to his head-piece; but, alas! when Mr. R—— went for them they were not to seen. Far and wide we looked, but not a trace of them could we find. It was truly despairing. We all separated to go in various directions. I wandered down by the creek and many a time did I think I discerned them in the distance and hurried on only to find it was a fallen tree or bunch of cattle. After wandering about for an hour I went back and found J—— and Mr. B—— had also been equally unlucky, but as Mr. R—— had not returned we trusted his search might be more successful. He was wonderfully well acquainted with the locality, and also with the ways of the animals—I suppose from long observation, and I often marvelled at and admired his great perception in these respects. The sick man and his friend had departed, and the man at the ranche was most anxious to give us breakfast. He was a young fellow, living quite alone, but so pleasant and friendly and with such natural good manners it was quite refreshing to meet him. I had a long chat about the country and its ways, whilst he made our coffee, baked some hot rolls, and fried bacon. He kept a store as well as a road ranche, and gave us a tin of delicious grapes, so we had quite a feast. J—— was just setting off in a backward direction, on the rancheman's pony, to see if our truant horses had made their way back to Big Powder River, when on the sky line of the horizon we saw them coming, Mr. R—— riding the little mare, the rest following.

Poor soul! he had had a long dreary chase after them, and Americans do not at all appreciate going on foot anywhere, and I don't think it improves their tempers when they have to do so. Mr. R—— gave some very short replies to our inquiries as to where and how he had come upon them, so we left him to refresh the inner man, and busied ourselves with rolling up the blankets, &c., and packing the traps—always a very tough job, as they had to be packed so close—and when all was ready we bade a warm farewell to the civil rancheman and started on our last day's drive.

Mr. R—— told me he had tracked the horses for some seven miles, and at last caught sight of them making for the top of a hill, led by the little mare. He hurried on and then whistled loudly to them. The little mare stopped, and then came towards him, and once she was caught, the rest followed. He felt very angry with them, he confessed, but that was all, as they were only following their natural instincts in trying to get to some place they knew out of a strange land. I felt very sorry that this was our very last day's drive. Never in my life had I enjoyed anything half so much as our wild rough life of the past few weeks. The delicious pure air, the scenery, the strange sights and experiences, the sense of utter freedom and independence, and, above all, the immunity from any ailment whatever—a feeling of such well-being that to rise in the morning was a delight and to live and breathe a positive luxury—made our few weeks' drive over the prairies a happy time for me to look back upon for all my life. I may be singular in this—it is more than possible I am, and that to most others the roughness, discomforts and the fatigue of such a journey would be an insuperable bar to any enjoyment in such an expedition—but I can only relate from my own experiences, and they were such as I describe.

The heat of this our last day, the 29th of June, was almost too intense to bear. The horses felt it greatly, and trotted along with drooping heads dejectedly. The road was quite good, as it was a well-worn track, and here and there we came upon cultivated patches of land, showing that the granger, that enemy to the cattleman, was at work. About noon we halted to water our horses at the ranche of a Dutchman, but could get no water as the spring was dried up, and they had to send some distance to bring what they needed for their own cattle; but they told us where we should find a spring further on. We were thankful for the shelter of their roof for a little while, and began to talk to the women of the place. Such funny little people! The old women with no shoes and stockings on, and all as lightly clad as was compatible with decency. They were full of a trip to Europe they meant to take at the fall of the year, and spoke of visiting London, Paris, Rome and other places. No doubt they would travel *en prince*, see everything, spend their pile, and return to their ranche life wiser, if poorer, than when they started. These good folk brought us some buttermilk, which we drank gratefully, and it tasted sweeter than the newest milk, and after halting for half-an-hour we drove on again for some miles till we reached the clump of trees that showed where the spring was. Such a delicious spot! The long grass growing luxuriantly and the water bubbling up and tumbling over the edge, making a deep little rivulet. J—— unharnessed his horses and drove them down the steep bank into the stream. The delight of the poor things was pleasant to see, as they stood up to their knees with their heads plunged in up to the eyes. Mr. R—— would not undo his pair, so he kept filling my gutta-percha foot-bath and handing it up for me to give them. It took a good many fillings before their thirst was appeased, poor beasts! and then we let them browse for a little on the lovely herbage.

But we were pressed for time, as we had a good bit of road to traverse before we could reach Miles City, our final destination. After driving some ten or twelve miles further on we came upon a very nice looking homestead, or rather I might call it a small village, as there was a cluster of ranches. We drove up to the largest, and for the first time, instead of waiting to undo my good Charlie, I hurried under shelter. My head was giddy with the heat and I felt utterly spent. The master of the house, seeing my sad plight, brought me some delicious milk with a lump of ice in it. It did surprise me greatly to find ice at these out-of-the-way places, but they store a lot in the winter time and it lasts well into the hot season. Ice is a real luxury, if not a necessity, in a country where sunstroke is by no means unknown, and a glass of iced milk restores one's failing energies far better than a brandy and soda or glass of wine would.

Our host busied himself in preparing some food for us, talking away all the time. We had got quite friendly by the time the horses were seen to and our men came in, and they, like me, were soon engaged in quaffing deep draughts of iced milk and water. The heat was so intense I can only compare it to being in the draught of a furnace. The breeze was hot and the sun blazing. I could not eat, so went and sat under some cotton trees by the stream, as the stove made the ranche stifling. I lay down for quite an hour, utterly exhausted. The poor dogs came and lay full length in the stream, and I rather wished to copy their example. I do not understand why heat strikes one as unsupportable in some climates, while in others, where the actual temperature may be higher, it does not seem to affect one to the same degree. I seldom even at Zanzibar or Aden felt so utterly prostrated by it; and it was with great reluctance we at last resumed our drive about six o'clock, having rested quite three hours. Our kind host seemed sorry to part from us, and we promised the next time we came by to stop the night—an easy promise to make, as it was most improbable we should ever be in that neighbourhood again.

The sun was getting low and a delicious breeze was rising as we slowly made our way over the baked hills and plains until, about half-past eight, we came in sight of the Yellowstone River, and here we drew up to admire quite the most gorgeous sunset I ever saw. Clouds of every colour from deepest purple to pale pink, and in the midst of them the sun sinking in a halo of blood-red light, the river looking like a golden streak between deep grey banks, and here and there a clump of cotton trees with their ghost-like white stems standing out in pale relief. We drove along in silence, gazing and gazing, till it all faded away into the dim twilight and then into the darker night, and presently the stars began to gleam here and there and later a pale clear moon; and so, in dusk and quiet, we drove into Miles City, to find lights gleaming in the windows of the numerous drinking saloons, and hoarse voices singing or shouting.

CHAPTER III

Back to Civilisation

OUR quiet lovely driving expedition was at an end; we had reached our final destination! There was only one hotel fit to stop at, so it was not difficult to find it, and we pulled up in front of a low wooden verandah about eleven at night. Mr. R—— went in, and presently returned, accompanied by the landlady and a coloured servant. We took off our luggage, leaving the bedding and rugs, and followed the man upstairs to a kind of parlour, opening on to the verandah on two sides, and then to our bed rooms—such quaint little box-like places, all opening on to the gallery, each room about twelve feet by ten—and, oh, the stifling heat of them! It was a wooden house, and the sun had been baking down upon the roof all day, till the rooms were really more like ovens than anything else. However, there was nothing to be done except open the door and window. As soon as I could I unpacked my box and got out a change of clothes, and then found my way to the bath room, which was down stairs and out of doors. The delight of that refreshing bath haunts me still. Certainly I had not enjoyed such a luxury for ten days, for the bath in the kitchen at Mr. Smith's ranche could hardly count. Of course, the men had bathed in the creeks and rivers on the way, often, as they said, coming out of the muddy water worse than when they went in. My dip in Big Powder River could not be called pleasant either, so I really revelled in the warm water, and felt so refreshed I could have started right off again that night.

I found J—— and Mr. B—— had followed my example, and we all assembled in the eating room waiting for something to eat to make its appearance. After nearly an hour the coloured waiter appeared carrying a tray with glasses of cold tea, some tough and very underdone bits of cold beef, some crackers and a jar of honey. It is quite contrary to American hotel rules to serve meals except at the fixed hours, and this was considered a very special favour.

After supper J—— found that by taking the 3:30 train that morning for Little Missouri he would quite save a day; and as this was an object with us, we being anxious to get back in time to catch the service, it was so settled, and he and Mr. B——, hastily putting a few things together, started for the train, leaving Mr. R—— and myself to manage for a few days as well as we could. I did feel so very sorry for them, they were both dead tired with the long day and the heat, and were counting on a good night's rest. Instead of this they had a weary railway journey of some hours, and not even a sleeping compartment, as these had been previously taken.

After seeing them off I returned to my oven, but finding it impossible to rest in such a stifling little den I carried my pillows and blankets on to the verandah and lay down till day broke. When I returned to my room, on examining our luggage, I found nearly all our clothes spoilt by the constant drenching they had undergone in muddy alkali rivers. I sent all to be washed by the Chinamen, and then paid half a dollar to have my boots cleaned. True, they were in a very bad state, but two shillings was pretty well. The thermometer registered 115° in the shade, and all day I simply sat in the verandah gasping, and with such a terrible headache. After sun down it got a little cooler, but I slept again on the verandah.

We were rather amused by the manners and customs of the "young ladies" who waited at the *table d'hôte*; they were even more free and easy than usual. I saw one of them quietly take a fan out of the hand of a man dining and begin to fan herself, leaning against the back of a chair all the time; and their insolent contempt of anything I asked them to do was very aggravating to my English feelings. Then, after supper, they came into the sitting room, bringing any friend they had, and talked and laughed as if the place belonged to them; and one of them, a rather pretty girl, used to don a riding habit and hat with a long feather, and go for a ride with her attendant cavalier. It was very funny, but not very comfortable.

We had almost settled to go into the Yellowstone Park before leaving for New York, but I received a note from J—— to say this was out of the question, as it would entail the purchase of a mule outfit and would take at least five weeks, and this we could not manage. I was not very sorry, as I was beginning to feel I had nearly come to the end of my endurance, and was anxious to get homeward.

On the 1st July J—— returned, having done what he had to do at Mr. Laing's ranche, and come into the middle of a very pretty quarrel.* But it is too long to relate at length; suffice it to say that the outcome of the dispute ended in the cold-blooded murder of a harmless old hunter by a foreign marquis, that both he and the old hunter's friend were arrested, that the marquis was admitted to bail and managed to get clear of it, as we learnt later, and the friend of the victim was punished, as, thanks to a very simple method, justice can be made to miscarry in a wonderful manner in these wild parts, where I am told every man has his price. But the affair caused a great stir at the time, and still rankles in the minds of the friends of the poor murdered man. With J—— came Mr. B—— and our old friend Mr. G——, who had come out West to try and make his fortune amongst the cattle and horse ranches, and who returned to Spearfish with Messrs. B—— and R——.

We spent that day in getting some photographs taken on the prairie of ourselves in our prairie attire, our horses and traps, and in packing our clothes; I also managed to get a few things I greatly needed for the journey—a tidy hat and veil and a linen ulster, or duster, as they are called, and some gloves, as we should not find our boxes till we got to Chicago, where they were sent when we left Cheyenne.

---

*[In the spring of 1883, Gregor Lang, representing John Pender, established a ranch on the Little Missouri River. One of his more colorful neighbors in the Little Missouri badlands was the Marquis de Mores, a French royalist and adventurer who was pursuing a grandiose scheme to make his newly created town of Medora (named after the marquise) a beef packing and shipping center. In a dispute with some local hunters over a fence he had built, De Mores shot and killed a man.]

The weather broke at last, and we had a tremendous thunderstorm, which cleared the air and made it cooler; but I still slept on the verandah. We had a great division of our boots, blankets, waterproof baths, &c., as there was no use in carrying them home; then I went to say good-bye to the horses. Charlie was always glad to see me, but Frank never got over his dislike to any handling—I suppose, from early reminiscences of a rough breaking—neither could I get him to care for sugar; the others all liked it. They had a long journey back before them, and I wished we also were driving back, instead of the three thousand miles of railroad we had to travel.

At two o'clock in the morning we were roused from our sleep, and hurried to the station. A chill, dull morning it was, and I think we all felt sad at the parting that must come. The train was punctual, and as the sun rose we steamed quietly out of Miles City, leaving three sad, wistful faces gazing after us till we were out of sight. I know I felt very sorrowful to think our long journey was over and our little band of comradeship dispersed for ever.

> We were a merrie companie, riding on land and sailing on sea,
> Oh, but we went merrilie;
> We forded the river, we climbed the high hill,
> And never a day our steeds stood still.

These lines kept running through my head, and it was not till we reached Mandan, where Mr. Laing met us with fresh accounts of the cruel murder, that I felt I could think of anything else. By this time the heat and dust had been terrible, and after we left Mandan we were glad of an excellent dinner served on the train, which helped to make one feel more cheerful, and as soon as we could we had the beds made up in our drawing-room car, and enjoyed a little sleep, which I stood really in great need of. We meant to have pushed on to Chicago, but I was feeling so done up and the heat was so intense, that we stopped for the night at St. Paul. I don't know really that we benefited much by this, as we found it a terribly hot place till a regular waterspout of rain came down about twelve at night, and this, as usual, cooled the air. We lost our drawing-room car also by stopping, and had to go on to Chicago in the ordinary sleeping Pullman, and as it was crowded, and a number of noisy children running about, the journey was very wearisome.

We reached Chicago about eight the next morning and drove to the Grand Pacific, a huge hotel, not uncomfortable, and with a splendid bath room attached to the bed room. I had a great day's work unpacking all our things and getting them separated for our visit to Newport; but it was a long business, as, of course, I had brought so much more than I need have done. We then went out to explore the town, and it certainly is wonderful to find it such a fine place, and to remember how lately it was burnt to the ground. We went on the same afternoon and travelled to a place called Shenandoah, which we reached at one in the morning, and had to get into the inn through the window, as we could not rouse the porter. He did not seem to mind, and took us up to a room with two beds in it, and the whole floor covered with plaster, a huge piece having fallen from the ceiling. However, we went to bed all the same, and were off by break of day next morning for Niagara, which place we spent the whole day exploring. I will not say anything about Niagara, as it is so well known. I am not quite clear about our route; I think

Shenandoah came after Niagara, but I was by this time feeling so ill and done up I did not keep my journal. I wanted greatly to see Niagara and also Lake George, so much spoken of in the annals of our history in America; so I did not allow that I was really ill, as we should have then gone on to New York. As we could not leave for England before the 18th, and as we were told that New York was simply intolerable from heat, I don't think I was very wrong.

Anyway, we had a lovely trip from Saratoga to Lake George, and I saw for the first time really finely wooded country. I had been much disappointed at the want of large fine trees such as one sees in English parks. Of course the firs, redwoods and pines are magnificent, but beech, oak and elm are small and scrubby.

Lake George is a lovely piece of water some 70 miles in length. There are numerous islands, and hotels and villas are being built all about. On one island was a camping-out party, and very merry they seemed. It is the fashion to make up a party, take tents, a stove, cooking utensils, &c., and to play at a Crusoe life on one of the lake islands, or on shore for the summer months, and a very pleasant time, no doubt, the young people have of it.

The steamer we went in was a very well appointed one and the food quite fair, and had I been well I should have greatly enjoyed the trip. We got to Albany and took a big river boat down the Hudson, and here I counted on a night's rest. The river boats are splendid to look at, all painted snow white, the cabins all white enamel, and such clean looking berths; but I found out to my cost it was all a delusion, as they simply swarm with the most hateful of insects, and I was driven out of the cabin and spent the night on a hard-backed bench, every available sofa or couch being taken up by travellers who had not engaged cabins. I spent a wretched night, and was thankful when we reached New York, which we did about six o'clock the following morning.

And here our trip may be considered at an end. We went to Newport, most delightful of watering-places, for a few days, stopping at a charming villa with our old friend Mr. R. Phelps, whose kindness to me I never can forget. (Alas, that we shall never meet again! He died the following year.) The thermometer at New York, on our return, registered 90 at midnight. It was most trying to an invalid such as I then was. We embarked on board the "Servia" on the 18th July and had a most perfect passage, the sea like a mill-pond the whole way, and we reached Queenstown early on the 26th, a fast passage of eight days.

And so ends the record of our most enjoyable four months' travels through the United States. We had seen, "done," and gone through as varied an experience as was possible in the time—an experience that I shall always look back upon as one of the most enjoyable of my life.